Groupwork Practice in Social Work

3rd Edition

Groupwork Practice in Social Work

Trevor Lindsay & Sue Orton

SAGE LearningMatters

Los Angeles | London | New Delhi
Singapore | Washington DC

Series Editors:
Jonathan Parker and Greta Bradley

Learning Matters
An imprint of SAGE Publications Ltd
1 Oliver's Yard
55 City Road
London EC1Y 1SP

SAGE Publications Inc.
2455 Teller Road
Thousand Oaks, California 91320

SAGE Publications India Pvt Ltd
B 1/I 1 Mohan Cooperative Industrial Area
Mathura Road
New Delhi 110 044

SAGE Publications Asia-Pacific Pte Ltd
3 Church Street
#10–04 Samsung Hub
Singapore 049483

Editor: Luke Block
Development editor: Lauren Simpson
Production controller: Chris Marke
Project manager: Diana Chambers
Marketing manager: Tamara Navaratnam
Cover design: Wendy Scott
Typeset by: Kelly Winter
Copy editor: Sue Edwards
Printed by Henry Ling Limited at
The Dorset Press, Dorchester, DT1 1HD

Library of Congress Control Number: 2014930443

British Library Cataloguing in Publication Data
A catalogue record for this book is available from the
British Library

ISBN 978-1-4462-8740-8 (hbk)
ISBN 978-1-4462-8741-5 (pbk)

Contents

About the authors

Trevor Lindsay draws on 35 years' experience of groupwork in the probation service and as a lecturer in social work. His practice experience includes specialised work with juvenile and adult offenders and across a range of settings. He has taught groupwork at qualifying and post-qualifying levels and has published a number of research articles in groupwork, group learning and criminal justice. He is the editor of *Social Work Interventions,* another title in this series. He is now retired from teaching but continues to write.

Sue Orton is an experienced educator and learning facilitator, with over 30 years' experience working in all sectors. She has qualifications and experience in Humanistic Psychology and Psychodrama and is also a Fellow of the Higher Education Academy. Sue now divides her time between supervising educators, trainers and coaches and her other passion, weaving. See www.sueorton.co.uk.

Preface to third edition

In this edition you will find two new sections. In teaching the groupwork method we have sometimes found that students have problems in imagining actual situations with service users where they could see themselves facilitating a group; even when students are in an actual practice setting and meeting with a particular group of service users, they can still experience difficulty in seeing how the method might be applied in that situation with that group of people. In Chapter 1, therefore, we have added in some examples of groupwork opportunities that present themselves with specific service-user populations in different settings.

Groupwork has long been recognised as having benefits for learning and, as a student, you will often find yourself in group learning situations. Additionally, while there are some difficulties presented by students being assessed in groups, lecturers may find that these can be overcome and that the advantages in terms of integrating learning and assessment, students learning from each other and developing useful skills of cooperation, collaboration, negotiation etc. outweigh any disadvantages. Consequently, in the chapter on group process (Chapter 5) we have included a new section in which, in addition to providing an illustration, we draw out from the discussion of *process* some pointers that we hope will be helpful to you when you find yourself learning or being assessed in a group.

The book has also been updated in line with the Professional Capabilities Framework for Social Work.

Acknowledgements

First, we would like to thank all the service users and students with whom we have had the temerity to practise. Second, we would like to acknowledge the contribution of the people with whom we have worked and who have influenced our thinking about the practice of groupwork, especially Kate Wilson of the University of Nottingham; John Burns (who devised the original Group Planner), formerly of Durham Probation and After Care Service; Cath Holmstrom and Pat LeRiche in the School of Social Work and Social Care at the University of Sussex; Hilary Burgess from the University of Bristol; Julia Phillips; former colleagues at SWAP; and Neill Thew, formerly head of Teaching and Learning Development at the University of Sussex. Third, thanks are due for their encouragement and support to friends in the Independent Practitioners Network: The Brighton Piers and to colleagues at the Social Work Department at the University of Ulster. We also would like to acknowledge the help and advice provided by Jonathan Parker and Lauren Simpson in the writing of the book.

Finally, we would like to acknowledge and thank our partners, Irene Lindsay and Sarah Quantrill, for their tremendous support and help. We dedicate this book to them.

Introduction

This book is a practical 'hands-on' guide to planning, setting up, facilitating and evaluating small helping groups, together with the theory that underpins them. Although primarily written for social work students, the book is also relevant for new groupworkers in other roles and professions, for example in education, youth work and community organisations, as well as in team management.

Both the social work degree and post-qualifying award in social work require that students are competent in working with groups, and such skills are also valuable in interprofessional practice, in partnership working and within the social care workforce. The book contains common-sense guidance on setting up, facilitating and closing small helping groups, and interprofessional and other groups. The reader is introduced to relevant skills by making links between personal experience and life skills, including the development of emotional intelligence, listening, questioning interventions and personal boundaries, then introduced to planning and preparation, the stages and decisions in groupwork, and guided through what to do when things seem to be going wrong.

Research (Trevithick, 2005a) suggests that groupwork as a subject warrants a higher profile within the social work degree in the UK. Trevithick (2006) makes the point that, in four out of the five areas of social work practice – work with families, groups, communities and organisations – an understanding of groupwork theory is clearly relevant. However, in the remaining area – work with individuals – it is equally relevant, since we cannot hope to understand individuals unless we also understand the groups to which they belong. We hope that this book might help this situation by encouraging more people to try groupwork, and experience and disseminate its benefits.

Requirements for social work education

The Professional Capabilities Framework (The College of Social Work, 2012) requires social workers to be able to:

> demonstrate a critical knowledge of the range of theories and models for social work intervention with individuals, families, groups and communities, and the methods derived from them; [to] select and use appropriate frameworks to assess, give meaning to, plan, implement and review effective interventions and evaluate the outcomes, in partnership with service users [and to] use a planned and structured approach, informed by social work methods, models and tools, to promote positive change and independence and to prevent harm.

Book structure

Chapter 1 introduces you to the concept of groups and the role these serve in human functioning. We discuss the characteristics of small helping groups and summarise the advantages, disadvantages and limitations of groupwork as a method of social work intervention and include some examples of social work populations for whom groupwork may be a helpful way of working.

Chapter 2 deals with planning your groupwork project: considering if a groupwork project is appropriate for meeting the identified yet unmet needs of service users and, if so, helping you make the case to colleagues in your organisation. We introduce the essential decisions in planning and structuring a group, taking into consideration issues of size, frequency, duration and composition, including age, class, ethnicity and gender.

Chapter 3 focuses on the tasks of facilitation: planning, intervening, monitoring and maintaining. We suggest that your facilitation style is grounded in your own values and principles and, more importantly, that your style will change and grow as you develop self-awareness. We offer models, theories and activities to assist your personal development, looking at intervention skills in some detail, including listening, questioning and six categories of intervention: supportive, catalytic, cathartic, confronting, informative and prescriptive. The chapter closes with a discussion of the pros and cons of co-facilitation, including factors that help a successful partnership.

Chapter 4 looks at the activities required when setting up the group, including the advantages of preliminary meetings with service users or potential group participants and what might be included in a groupwork contract.

Chapter 5 addresses group processes. Knowledge of how groups behave is important not only in making planning decisions, but also in making sense of what is going on. You will learn of some theoretical explanations of group processes and develop an understanding of how groups change and develop over time. We also argue that knowledge of process will be helpful to you as a student when you are learning as a member of a student group or being assessed through groupwork.

Chapter 6 leads on to how knowledge of process will be useful in planning a programme of activities for the group. You will read about the advantages of having a programme and learn about some of the issues to be taken into account in deciding on the shape of each session. We provide examples that you can adapt to suit your group.

Chapter 7 deals with issues of power and oppression. Recognising that your group will be representative of a society where power is not evenly shared and is used to oppress people, you will be introduced to the different aspects of anti-oppressive practice that need to be borne in mind at every stage of the facilitation role. You will consider how you might prepare yourself as an anti-oppressive facilitator, in terms of your awareness of yourself, and being able to recognise and deal with oppressive behaviour.

Chapter 8 discusses some of the challenges you may face in terms of unexpected and unhelpful responses from both those in the group and those outside it. We introduce you to some of the difficulties that can arise and you will be encouraged to adopt an analytical approach to identifying the causes. Having read the chapter you will have some ideas about the responses you may make. You will be introduced to the idea of having a mentor.

Chapter 9 considers the tasks needed to gather evidence about your groupwork projects in order to demonstrate success to the different audiences and stakeholders, to enable you to learn and develop your practice and to disseminate your findings. We advocate developing a systematic approach to monitoring, recording and evaluating your groupwork before, during and after your project.

Learning features

As with the other books in this series, this book is interactive. You are encouraged to work through the book as an active participant, taking responsibility for your learning, in order to increase your knowledge, understanding and ability to apply this learning to practice. You will be expected to reflect creatively on how your learning needs can be met with respect to working with groups and how your professional learning can be developed for your future career.

Case studies throughout the book will help you to examine theories and models for social work practice. These are mostly fictionalised versions of real events we have encountered in practice. Activities that require you to reflect on experiences, situations and events will help you to review and summarise learning undertaken. In this way your knowledge will become deeply embedded as part of your development. When you come to practise learning in an agency, the work and reflection undertaken here will help you to improve and hone the skills and knowledge needed for your groupwork. Suggestions for further reading will be made at the end of each chapter.

Terminology

You will find in this book that we refer to facilitator, groupworker, worker and conductor. We use these terms interchangeably. A theme throughout the book is our insistence that, at its best, groupwork is an empowering, participative, integrating method of working with service users. As such, we eschew the use of the term 'leader', preferring to talk of conducting, facilitating and working with groups, rather than leading them. This is not to say that we deny the power and responsibility inherent in the role, that we do not recognise the centrality of the position that a facilitator occupies, or that we do not understand that most of the professional knowledge, skills and values needed to ensure the success of the group are located in that role. We do, however, wish to acknowledge that, at times, the leadership role can pass to other individuals in the group, that we wish to encourage the conditions in which this can happen successfully, and that all the members of the group, including the facilitators, are equal and that the group belongs to them all in equal measure.

Chapter 1
What is groupwork?

A C H I E V I N G   A   S O C I A L   W O R K   D E G R E E

This chapter will help you to develop the following capabilities from the Professional Capabilities Framework.

- **Professionalism**
  Identify and behave as a professional social worker, committed to professional development.
- **Knowledge**
  Apply knowledge of social sciences, law and social work practice theory.
- **Critical reflection and analysis**
  Apply critical reflection and analysis to inform and provide a rationale for professional decision-making.
- **Intervention and skills**
  Use judgement and authority to intervene with individuals, families and communities to promote independence, provide support and prevent harm, neglect and abuse.

It will also introduce you to the following academic standards as set out in the Quality Assurance Agency (QAA) social work subject benchmark statement.

5.1.1 Social work services, service users and carers
5.1.4 Social work theory
5.5.4 Intervention and evaluation

Introduction

So you want to work with groups? If you are reading this book as a student on a social work degree, you may be worried about your ability to meet course requirements for working with groups. Groupwork is at the core of social work, but what is it? Is it different from sitting round a table with your friends planning a party? Yes, probably, but in what ways? You *do* need to behave differently, but how and what does it mean for you? It is a lot more serious, since people's lives are involved. For one thing, you hold much more responsibility for planning and outcomes. Groupwork and group facilitation can also be a bit scary. Why might that be? Some reasons occur to us immediately. It will be rather more obvious to rather more people if we make a mess of it. Perhaps it feels risky too in terms of being challenged, put on the spot by the group members, with our ignorance or lack of skill exposed. So how do we go about learning to organise and facilitate groups in a way that meets our responsibilities to the service users, our colleagues and our supervisors?

Our intention here is to help you to:

- begin to answer some of these questions;

- understand the contexts, challenges and situations you may meet;

- acknowledge the behaviour, skills and experience that you will need to bring to the front of your awareness;

- start planning, participating in and facilitating groupwork.

What is a group?

ACTIVITY **1.1**

Spend a few minutes thinking about the groups of which you are currently a member. Write them down on a piece of paper.

COMMENT

How many did you get? Did you include family groups? You, your partner and children? Your parents and brothers and sisters? Your extended family? Social groups? Friends you meet up with at college? at gigs? after work? What about work groups, team meetings, trade union groups, task groups, committees? recreational groups? sports, music, reading, dieting? educational groups, buzz groups, seminar groups, presentation groups, study groups? It is clear that much of what we do, we do in groups.

We must first start by trying to establish some idea of what actually *is* a group. This is perhaps an equally difficult concept.

Some questions to ask

- How small or large can a group be and yet still be considered a group?

- We would agree that two people are not a group, but are three?

- What about 12, or 28?

- How long do people in a group have to have known each other to be a group?

- How regularly do they have to meet?

- Do they always meet in the same place?

- Do they have to meet at all or is it enough just to believe that you are a member of a group, even if it never meets, communicating perhaps over the internet, and being aware of the other people as a group?

- Who is it who is to say that a group exists? Is the group defined by people outside it who can say 'Look, there is a group', or does the group have to be aware of its existence as a group?

Perhaps it is impossible to arrive at a definition of a group since groups do not exist necessarily as separate definable entities. Phillips (2006) argues that trying to define the term is of little use to anyone. Manor (2000) makes the interesting point that every group has some unique features, yet all groups have characteristics that are the same. Perhaps we can make a stab at some of the qualities that any group has, that allow us to recognise it as a group, either as observers or participants. Many writers have attempted this. Preston-Shoot (2007) suggests that a necessary condition is that there is a collection of people who spend time together and that they both recognise themselves as a group and are seen by other people as a group. Levine and Moreland (2006) suggest that it may be misguided to make hard-and-fast distinctions between *groups* and *nongroups*, preferring to think in terms of *groupiness, or social interaction, as a dimension along which sets of people can vary* (p2). *Groupiness*, they explain, is greater in sets of people who interact more frequently and intensively, and have an idea of a group history and future. Coulshed and Orme (2006) argue that a perception of group membership extends beyond the time that the people spend together. Being a member of a group involves loyalty and commitment, which arise out of the interaction that takes place. They suggest that indeed members of internet 'chat rooms' may well consider themselves to be members of a group and that it is not therefore necessary that the group physically meets. Brown (1992) adds to the concept the ideas that there is interdependence between the members and that some common purpose exists, however ill-defined. Groups can be either formal or informal. A group may be a collection of young people who hang around a bus stop or it could be a committee set up by a government body.

Social, family and informal groups

Our starting place is your experience of groups and for you to reflect on your behaviour and 'roles' in those groups – first in the social, family and informal gatherings, of which you will have direct experience already, and then in 'working' groups – and to see what makes them different. We will then consider how these reflections might link you to social work groupwork.

There are groups that you are joined to because of your life circumstances. Think how you are in those groups, how you behave, and how safe or unsafe you feel when contributing or getting your voice heard. Think of the behaviour or 'roles' that are played in the group and how they affect your own behaviour. Reflect on these matters when you next join such a group. There is no right or wrong here, but there is value in building awareness of your and other people's behaviour and intentions when in these groups. Why? Because it is likely that you might transfer some of the behaviours, reactions or your unspoken 'rules' from these groups into 'groupwork' groups, especially when you start to facilitate them.

ACTIVITY *1.2*

Can you think of an occasion when you behaved in a work group in a way that you have behaved in your family group? We are thinking, perhaps, of 'family rules' from the past that we still trip over in other situations in which we have to remind ourselves that we can behave differently now.

Now look at groups that you have chosen to join around an interest, life preference or social gathering. How are you in these groups? Are your behaviour, sense of safety and level of contribution different from those you experience in family or work groups? If so, how and why do you think that is?

Writing or drawing will help you build the picture.

COMMENT

Again, there is no right or wrong here, and the reason for building your awareness is the same. You are painting a picture of you in groups.

Working groups

The term *group* covers a wide range of gatherings and forms, from long-term training, seminars and workshops, to formal and informal meetings and gatherings, and personal and therapeutic development groups. The *work* bit may suggest a purpose. The interesting question is what the 'work' is and who does it. What are the factors that enable the work to happen in a clear, supportive and honest way? What role does the leader or facilitator of a group have? Who sets the rules for what should happen when? One of the keys is the relationship between the intention or purpose of the group and the behaviour that results.

Again, you may be familiar with groups that have been formed for a specific issue or purpose. Maybe you have attended or participated in a school council, a residents' meeting, or a society annual general meeting; think of examples of groups you have seen, joined or participated in with a set agenda or reason for gathering.

- Who decides when and where they meet?
- How do they organise themselves and know what to do?
- Is there an agenda or order of business?
- How do they decide who speaks when and what happens if these 'rules' are broken?

There will be a link between the behaviour(s) of participants and the agenda or purpose of the gathering. Can you think of examples of this link? If you can, what are they? Perhaps discuss this with your friends and colleagues.

You might also find watching television reality shows or parliament or your local council meeting helpful for developing very different insights into groups 'working'. As in the previous section, note your feelings and responses to watching different groups. Watch how people behave and consider the intention behind their behaviour. Could they have chosen to behave in a different way? What do you notice? What processes, feelings or emotions are involved in dealing with the issues? Emotion will be around, but usually not as an acknowledged and valued part of the decision-making process. Looking for clues in your emotional responses will be useful for developing facilitation skills later. Take reality shows. What is the intention? To get you hooked, yes, but why and how do they do it? It may be something to do with anticipating the 'risky' or 'free' behaviour of participants. They may be saying or doing things that you would never dare to do but might like to if you had the nerve. If you watch them, what is your reaction and does it link to your experience in groups? If you do not watch reality TV shows, why not? Are there clues for you about your experience of acceptable and non-acceptable behaviour?

We all react differently to different circumstances in groups and it is almost entirely due to our own personal responses and choices. You may be unconscious or sceptical of the idea of choosing behaviour at first but you will become more conscious of your choices with experience.

Small helping groups – groupwork

Most people when they come across the word 'groupwork' probably have some preconceived idea of what it is, perhaps taken from films such as *One Flew Over the Cuckoo's Nest* or television. Generally, it brings up an image of a group of people sitting around on hard chairs in a circle looking very uncomfortable. You probably have a much better idea. You may have worked with groups in the past or have yourself been a member of a small helping group. It may seem obvious to start by saying that groupwork is working with groups, but beyond that it is a term that is hard to define.

From the exercise (Activity 1.1) above, it should have become clear to you that, as a fairly average human being (if we may dare suggest that you are average, which, of course, you are not), you are a member of a number of different groups and in fact have been operating in groups now for quite a long time. Being in a group, then, is a fundamental part of human existence. Like many other animals, we are group creatures. Why should this be? Since being in groups is such a universal phenomenon, it must provide us with a number of benefits. Being in a group must have advantages for us.

ACTIVITY **1.3**

We are going on now to discuss some of the benefits that groups can have, but, before we start, there is some work for you to do to get you thinking about this. List reasons why, for you, being in groups is beneficial.

COMMENT

Some of us take greater benefit out of being in groups than others. Although we have absolutely no evidence, other than personal experience, to back this up, we would say that people who like being in groups are likely to feel more comfortable as group facilitators than those who do not. It is important to be aware of the benefits that groups have for us and for others.

Attractions and benefits of groups

There are a number of reasons why people are attracted to groups, for example the safety provided by numbers and the opportunities to trade or pool resources and share ideas. However, the benefits are even more significant than this. As Douglas (1978, p3) says, *our need of other people is absolutely basic to our continued existence*. We can really only be sure of our existence through our interaction with other people.

Feedback

It is only by attending to how other people react to us that we are able to develop a sense of ourselves. However, during our lifetime, because we engage with countless numbers of people, the mass of unstructured feedback we get can be too varied to be of any use to us. For feedback to be of value to us it must be regular, frequent and consistent, and we must be willing and able to understand it. To begin to get feedback, we need to get close enough to a number of people who are happy to be that close to us. But more than that, the groups that will tolerate us as members will, over time, provide us with the consistent, frequent, predictable feedback that we need to form a sense of ourselves.

ACTIVITY **1.4**

List some of the feedback you have 'gathered' from friends and family. It may be positive or negative!

COMMENT

Consider your response to the different feedback. Do you hear or expect the positive or negative? Which do you find yourself willing to hear and accept? Sometimes we expect the negative and can find it more difficult to accept the positive. For others, it may be the other way round. Generally speaking, we are better at owning positive feedback. Negative feedback is harder to take and most of us have well-constructed defence mechanisms that allow us to deny or rationalise negative feedback away. This is why it is better to give negative feedback in the form of how a person might improve rather than how they did not do well. We will return to this in later chapters.

What is groupwork as a social work method?

We have seen that we live in groups and depend on groups for our sense of ourselves. It seems obvious that, when we set out to help other people, working with them in groups makes sense.

So, having established that group experience is fundamental and therefore an obvious choice when intervening to help people, it should be possible for us to define what we mean by groupwork, in the sense that we mean it as a social work method. For the purpose of this book, therefore, we have arrived at the following definition of groupwork for social work. It draws on a number of sources (Benson, 2001; Brown, 1992; Konopka, 1963, cited in Brown, 1992).

Groupwork: a working definition

Social groupwork is a method of social work that aims, in an informed way, through purposeful group experiences, to help individuals and groups to meet individual and group needs, and to influence and change personal, group, organisational and community problems.

For our purposes here, we are going to concentrate on groups that have been especially set up by a social worker with the intention of intervening in a way that is helpful to the individual, group, organisation or community. That is, groups that have been brought together for a particular beneficial purpose and that meet at a specified time and place. Social workers do engage with groups in a number of other situations. Examples would include pre-existing groups, such as groups of young people in the community who are seen as creating problems, groups that occur as a consequence of the existence of some particular setting but are not specifically constructed as helping groups, such as house meetings for the residents in a hostel, or groups whose existence is transitory or fleeting, such as a group that has met at a community centre for some reason of its own. Groups such as these do offer opportunities for help, but they are not our focus here. That is not to say that our discussion is irrelevant in working with them – on the contrary. We are able to use our definition to include groups that are not attended entirely voluntarily, such as groups of offenders. We also wish to begin to introduce the concept of facilitation or shaping and leading groupwork as we consider the range of reasons why groups can help.

Why can groups help?

RESEARCH SUMMARY

Meta-analysis is a research method that examines a number of individual research studies in an attempt to resolve the confusion that arises from different studies measuring different effects and arriving at differing or even contradictory conclusions. It helps to give an overall picture of a number of different studies on the same topic. Burlingame et al. (2003, cited in Coyne and Diederich, 2013) conducted a meta-analysis of 111 studies of groupwork projects and found that the average group client improved more than 72 per cent of controls who were untreated.

Being in groups is a normal part of our lives

It seems obvious that, since we spend much of our time in groups in the natural course of things, it may be helpful to work with people in groups so that they are provided with an opportunity to improve that part of their human functioning. Skills that individuals develop in working with others in the group, for example in communicating, relationship-building and asserting oneself, can be transferred to their lives outside.

People with similar life experiences, situations and problems can be a source of support to each other

People who have had particularly damaging and hurtful experiences, or who are at present experiencing very difficult situations, often either feel isolated and alone or are prevented by their situation from joining with others. Included here might be those who have recently lost a close relative, or who are coping with their partner's substance misuse (Al-Anon being an excellent example). Meeting up with other people who have had similar experiences may therefore be a great source of help as they come to realise that their situations are not so unique. Feelings of guilt can be dissipated and cognitive difficulties associated with the experience can be overcome. People sharing similar life experiences are able to share the emotions that arise in them and in this way come to realise that these emotions are both normal and valid. Rogers (1957) tells us that the sense of being accepted as we are is one of the essential conditions for personal growth. Service users who are seen alone can, of course, develop this sense of acceptance from their interaction with their social worker, but having the acceptance and respect of a number of their peers can be a much more powerful experience and greatly increase feelings of self-worth.

Groupwork can be empowering

Generally speaking, social workers and social care staff are in relatively more powerful positions than the people with whom they work. This can be because of the statutory power given to the agency, by the resources that it holds or simply because of the knowledge and information held by the worker. In a one-to-one situation, this puts the service user very much at the weaker end of the power equation. However, in a group, the worker's power can be balanced by the power that comes to the group members because of their greater numbers. One of us (Trevor) came to groupwork as a consequence of dissatisfaction in working with teenage offenders on a one-to-one basis, finding it very boring and unproductive for both worker and client, but, when faced with a group of very vocal and disaffected young people, quickly had to find ways of working with, rather than against, the young people. Groupworkers who wish to impose their will upon the group, or who represent agencies that require attendance and compliance, can have a more difficult time in their work with groups. Time can be spent negotiating issues concerned with power and control, without necessarily bringing any benefit to the group members. These issues are, of course, of concern in any small helping group, but where groupworkers are free to enter into a more equal dialogue with the group members it is possible, even likely, that this process will help with the group's development. Groupwork may appeal to workers who prefer a more democratic, empowering and participatory approach to their work.

Empowerment comes through being able to understand how the problem lies outside the individual and results from oppressive policies, practices, behaviours and the ideas on which these are founded. Any therapeutic experience can be considered a potentially empowering process, but particularly when clients are put in touch with the resources available to them and encouraged to take responsibility for their own choices and improvement. In groups, bringing people together to help and support each other is in itself empowering, but it also greatly adds to the resources that then become available through the others in the group. People who come together as a consequence of having similar problems or concerns then find themselves in a position where they can collectively confront these forces of oppression, in ways that they could not do single-handedly. Doel and Sawdon (1999) include a useful chapter on power and empowerment in groupwork, in which they state that *Empowerment, in the sense of an increasing feeling of self-worth and a growing ability to feel and use power in constructive ways, should be an integral part of the members' experience of the group* (p51).

Groups offer opportunities for giving and receiving help

This advantage arises again out of the numerical facts. In a group, each member has a number of other people available who can offer support, advice and suggestions. A vast range of experience is brought to bear on problems and situations. It is important to realise that it is as beneficial to have opportunities to give help, as it is to receive it. This can be of crucial importance to people who, due to their difficulties, have been labelled previously as being worthless or inadequate, and whose self-esteem is at a low ebb. Not only does it provide an emotional boost and increased feelings of worth, but also the opportunity to get away from one's own problems by helping with another's.

RESEARCH SUMMARY

Hopmeyer and Werk (1993) conducted a study of four family bereavement groups. They found that 40 per cent of the respondents felt that they had given and received help in equal measure in their group.

Groups offer opportunities for social comparison

People in groups are exposed to a range of different ways of behaving. We have discussed above the potential that groups have for the normalisation of the feelings that arise out of a shared experience. We can take this idea a little further. Even if people do nothing but observe, they will be experiencing the behaviours of others. Some of these will be familiar and some not. Feelings may be expressed by other members of the group that individuals themselves would never dare to express. Carers are supposed to be very kind, loving, patient and *caring*, but, of course, no one is like that, at least not all the time. Button (1997) suggests that groups have the capacity to hold 'big feelings' such as shame, terror and rage. He suggests that a common factor in the thwarted expression of big feelings is the sense of those feelings being unmet, unheard or unseen. Many carers have that experience. An important function of a group can be for these feelings to be met, heard and seen by a number of people in a safe and valued way. People may also find that beliefs they have and hold are not the beliefs that others have, and that some people do not accept their 'given truths' at all. In theory, this aspect of being in a group could bring about a negative experience; for example, someone may feel that everyone else is much more confident, articulate or able to express feelings than he or she is. However, Whitaker (1985) argues that this will not happen if the group manages to get down to the fundamentals of human experience. It is at this level that we share a common experience of feelings of anger, fear, sorrow and joy and a desire for close relationships.

Groups offer learning opportunities

Some groups are established with the main aim of providing information. For example, drug and alcohol education programmes aim to increase participants' awareness of the physical, biological and psychological effects of substance misuse. However, to use a group simply to impart information in an economic way is a poor use of the medium and misses out on many of the advantages of group learning. Jaques (2000) provides a comprehensive discussion of groups for learning.

- **Groups provide variety in available learning methods.** Groupwork provides opportunities to use a variety of learning methods not normally available to the individual worker. Group activities and exercises can be delivered that will cater for the learning styles of every individual. All sorts of activity, for example trust games, relationship exercises, simulations, role-plays and sculpts, can be introduced to provide a range of learning experiences, and many of these are experienced by the group members as being exciting and enjoyable as well as informative and helpful.

- **Group members have the opportunity to learn from each other.** This can happen in a number of ways. First, people who share problems can learn from others about effective ways of dealing with the situations that arise. People who, for example, are looking after a dependent relative find it useful to come together to discuss their situation and to share solutions to some of the problems that they encounter. Second, there is also the possibility of learning from each other through a process of discovery. Learning can come about in a way that is more natural and meaningful, through discussion and exploration of ideas. Being able to arrive at solutions through discovery with others can promote deeper learning than being presented with a 'ready-made' solution. Opportunities for personal growth are offered also by the opportunities to observe the behaviour of others and to learn from it. Additionally, individuals are able to see what the outcomes are of the behaviour of the other group members, for example what happens if someone challenges the facilitator or another group member.

- **A group provides opportunities for acquiring information about how one's behaviour is experienced and responded to by others.** In groups, feedback can be more powerful, since it comes from a number of people who are in similar situations or perhaps of a similar age, ethnicity, class, and so on. Button (1997, p6) suggests that groups offer *a multifaceted mirror for reflection and feedback.* People are able to see how others relate to each other and what responses they get. All social situations provide individuals with feedback, in the sense that all behaviour has consequences that occur in the form of a response to that behaviour. In groups, the amount of feedback is increased. Particular activities can be provided that will encourage the members of the group to provide feedback and the feedback may be underlined or made more explicit, so that it can be utilised to help individuals learn about the impact of their behaviour on others, and perhaps re-examine their actions in the light of this.

- **A group offers opportunities for trying out new behaviours.** A group can provide a safe environment in which people can experiment with behaviour that is new to them or try out solutions that had not previously occurred to them. This could occur in a contrived scenario, such as rehearsing for a forthcoming job interview or practising asserting themselves in a simulation of a situation in which they have never been able to assert themselves in the past. Alternatively, it can occur in a more spontaneous way as they dare to express an emotion that they ordinarily keep to themselves.

Groups provide hope and optimism

The belief in the possibility of improvement is a major factor in recovery, should it be from a physical illness, an emotional difficulty or a practical problem. The stronger the belief that one can succeed, the more likely it is to happen. This effect is often referred to as 'self-efficacy', a construct introduced by Bandura (1995) and that he defines as *a belief in one's capabilities to organise and exercise the courses of action required to manage prospective situations* (p2). Groupwork offers ways in which self-efficacy is increased. The very fact that a number of people come together to work on a problem suggests that there is hope that the problem can be remedied, since presumably they would not bother if this was not the case. Similarly, as group members observe each other in the process of solving their problems or hearing how they have solved problems in the past, they take heart that they too will be able to do this in the future. The role of the facilitator is of crucial importance and self-efficacy is unlikely to develop if the facilitator does not also firmly believe that positive change is possible and likely. The facilitator also has an important role to play in building self-efficacy in the group, for example by emphasising members' strengths and capacity to change, and by providing information or examples of successes in this group or in other groups.

Groups can offer a way of reaching the unreachable

Some people can be quite difficult to reach using individual methods, but may be happier to obtain help through membership of a group. People can be quite suspicious of the motives of individual social workers. In child protection, for example, the service user may fear that the social worker plans to remove a child from its family. For others, the social distance with a social worker may be too great for them to be able to contemplate any trust or closeness in an individual relationship. Disaffected young people may not be prepared to relate to an individual social worker, or perhaps feel that they would face ridicule from their peers if they did, but nevertheless may be happy to meet in a group and even consider it 'cool'.

ACTIVITY **1.5**

Your team has decided to set up a group for young people of both genders, who come from an area of high deprivation and with a range of social problems. Young people living in the area are at risk of drug misuse, joyriding and other crime. The aim of the group would be to try to reduce risk-taking behaviour. How might you increase the 'coolness' factor in the group?

CASE STUDY

Probation officers in Belfast run a group that aims to reduce sectarianism in young men of both religions. The group focuses on football, not only playing the game but also using it as material for learning. One session, for example, uses football symbolism (badges, shirts, scarves) to draw parallels with sectarian symbolism (flags, badges, kerb-painting, murals).

COMMENT

In this example we can see that the facilitators, recognising that the theme of anti-sectarianism would be unlikely to be an attractive one to the potential group members, found a topic that would be, but that also would lend itself to drawing comparisons that could be put to use. They did not make any attempt, of course, to disguise the actual aim of the group, but they provided an activity that would be attractive to the group members and also provided them with a reason for attending that would be considered legitimate by family and friends.

Groupwork can be an economical way of helping

It may seem rather obvious to say that, since we can have contact with a number of service users at once, groupwork can be a more economical way of working. However, we need to approach this idea with some caution for a number of reasons. First, groupwork can be a more complex way of working and this can mean that we need to spend a greater amount of time in planning, arranging for the group to take place, and later thinking about and analysing what took place. This complexity may result in our decision to use two or more facilitators rather than just one. While this may be good practice, it can add another level of complexity. For this, we need to allow more time, as the facilitators communicate and discuss not only the dynamics in the group, but also their own relationship and their part in facilitation. Another issue is that the individuals in the group may continue to need one-to-one attention in addition to the groupwork sessions. A person who is attending a group due to problems with alcohol or drugs may also need to continue to see a social worker outside the group, for example because of particular problems in his or her family. So although, in certain situations, some economies may sometimes be available, it is best not to see groupwork as a time-saving alternative to individual work, but to see both approaches as offering different advantages and being supplementary to each other.

The advantages of groupwork as a helping method are covered comprehensively and in some detail in both Whitaker (1985) and Brown (1992).

Advantages for facilitators

The motivation to set up and facilitate groups does not have to be entirely altruistic. As a method of social work, groupwork also has certain advantages for the facilitators and we wish to discuss these briefly at this point.

Our experience is that people work better when they anticipate some reward. Research by Herzberg et al. (1959) found that the most important motivators in work were a sense of achievement, recognition and the work itself.

We have already discussed the advantages offered for learning. Many of these benefits are as available to the facilitators as they are to the group members. Social work and other students may also find that groupwork offers them particularly rich opportunities to collect evidence of their abilities and their competence to satisfy examiners. Some beginning workers can find it a more comfortable medium in which to work and others may even find it fun! Finally, we should also recognise that it sometimes provides workers with kudos. It can be considered a more innovative and creative way of working and therefore carries some prestige. Of course, these are not necessarily the best of reasons for embarking on a groupwork project; the first consideration should always be to try to meet the needs of the service users, but it is right that we should acknowledge that these advantages to the worker also exist.

Possible limitations of groupwork

It would be disingenuous of us not to make it quite clear that there are some potential disadvantages to groupwork and that for some people it is not a good way of working. There are also social workers and care workers for whom groupwork may not be a comfortable working method. Davies (1975) suggests the following limitations.

Groupwork is strange

Although groupwork is much more common today than it was when Davies was writing in 1975, it is still seen as a minority interest in some situations (Ward, 2002). The consequences of this are twofold. First, it can result in an unsympathetic agency environment, where colleagues approach the method from a position of suspicion or ignorance, perhaps even envy. Second, it can mean a consequential lack of support within the agency, which in turn can result in work that is inadequately prepared or evaluated. The circle is completed when the outcome of this is increased scepticism.

Groups can become self-obsessed

As individuals in the group find common concerns, goals and a sense of identity, they can come to value this over all else. For some people the main concern becomes the group itself: its survival, its reputation, its cohesiveness and its control over its members. This can even take priority over the needs or the welfare of individual members. In these circumstances, people in the group or outside it can get hurt. Some groups become so inward-looking that they lose some sense of reality. Groupworkers need to work hard to keep a sense of reality by linking the group experience to what is happening outside.

CASE STUDY

A social worker attended a three-day residential course, in which most of the time was spent in a base group. This group became extremely close and the members spent much of their time together discussing problems they were having with their organisations, particularly their managers, supporting each other and coming up with possible solutions. On returning to work, the social worker immediately challenged the team leader in a very emotional and direct way, with obvious consequences for their relationship.

COMMENT

In this example the group had been so powerful that the social worker had carried the overwhelming emotions raised in the experience over into everyday life, and had not been able to make the adjustment necessary to take the concerns forward in a more diplomatic and effective way.

Brown (1992) adds the following to the disadvantages above, identified by Davies.

The individual is likely to get less undivided attention

It follows that it is difficult for a group to cater for all the needs of all the group members at the same time as providing the same attention as each might expect from individual contact. It is important, therefore, that the facilitator has a continuing awareness of the needs of each individual as well as of the whole group. At times, however, it is possible for a skilled facilitator to provide for the needs of one individual in a way that is of benefit to all, for example in dealing with a problem that is a major concern for one but is shared by the others. The member who brings to the group a difficult relationship with her mother provides the opportunity for others to disclose similar problems and to find a common solution. The knack is to keep the discussion of interest to everyone. It is not appropriate to focus exclusively on one member. Nevertheless, there may be some people who could not possibly cope with sharing and competing in a group due to their particular circumstances, or whose problems require a great deal of individual work and who cannot really benefit from a group until they have moved on to some degree. People who have experienced a sudden recent bereavement, for example, may not yet have sufficiently resolved or come to terms with what has happened to them to be able to listen to the experiences of others, or discuss their own. The facilitator needs to make a decision about how helpful or otherwise the group might be for such a person.

No guarantees of confidentiality can be given

Confidentiality can be even more of an issue when working with groups than in one-to-one work, simply because there are more people involved and listening to what is being said.

CASE STUDY

A social worker was running a group for isolated women. Roberta, a member of the group, had joined as a result of being referred by a colleague social worker. The groupworker was very surprised when Roberta became extremely angry: her complaint was that the groupworker had repeated something to the colleague that Roberta had said in the group. The groupworker could not understand this anger; the information passed on was not of particular significance or sensitivity; in fact, it was common knowledge. Surely, Roberta knew that the groupworker would be talking to the social worker colleague? The reason for Roberta's anger was not the disclosure of this particular information but the fact that the groupworker had communicated with the colleague at all. The group had not been made aware that this would happen.

COMMENT

People can rarely be given absolute guarantees of confidentiality by their social workers, who have responsibilities to protect other members of society as well as their clients, but at least they can spell out the limits of their confidentiality. Members of groups have to rely on the discretion of all the other members as well as the facilitators, and have to be informed that the risk of their confidentiality being breached, while undesirable, is always present.

Groups can be complex and expensive to plan and implement

We have mentioned already the extra work that needs to be undertaken in planning and facilitation tasks. To this needs to be added the work that must be done with employing agencies and one's colleagues to ensure that the project is properly supported. Most groups require the allocation of resources in addition to staff time, whether this is a space to meet (which can often present a major hurdle) or something as simple as the provision of tea and coffee.

Groups can be harmful for some

There are a number of ways in which membership of a group can prove harmful to an individual. Belonging to a small helping group can add to stigmatisation. The users of social work services are often already stigmatised and labelled as a consequence of their problems. Membership of a group aimed specifically at addressing these problems can add to the stigma and the group may be conducted at a venue that in itself also carries a stigma. Often people with problems have a considerable need to be regarded as normal and will not wish to be labelled even more firmly.

Whitaker (2001) includes a chapter on other situations where there is no gain or where there is actual harm. These include situations where:

• one person is more vulnerable than the others and is threatened or attacked;

• one person is conspicuously different from the others and is stereotyped or oppressed;

- the group adopts a collusive defence that requires one member to occupy a role that is harmful to them – Whitaker uses the example of the group requiring a member to occupy the role of substitute facilitator and then using this as a focus for anger and attack, displaced from being focused on the worker;

- an individual is excluded or ignored;

- a group member is drawn into experiencing unbearable feelings with which he or she does not have the resources to cope. An example here might be where a group starts discussing the corporal punishment of children. Unknown to them one member was repeatedly and severely beaten throughout his early life but has managed to deal with this by burying it deeply. The member becomes uncontrollably distressed and runs out of the group.

As Brown (1992) points out, many of these scenarios may not be illustrations of the limitations of groupwork, but provide indicators for protecting some people from unsuitable groups, or are pointers about issues of which we as facilitators need to be aware. A further interesting point needs to be borne in mind. As devotees of the groupwork method, we do not wish to appear to be too defensive here, but it is worth noting that social workers doing one-to-one work do not usually have to justify why they are working individually. The limitations of individual work are rarely enunciated.

Who can groups help?

Categorisation of populations for whom groupwork may be helpful

Whitaker (2001) provides a useful categorisation of groups of people for whom groupwork may be helpful. This is reproduced and amplified below in Table 1.1, with examples of the settings in which these populations may be found. This is included as students sometimes find it useful to have some indication of the opportunities for groupwork that are presented by these practice learning settings.

Please refer to the *Further reading* section at the end of this chapter for a list of material that focuses on groupwork with particular populations.

The tasks of facilitation

One common factor in all the examples is that the group needs to be steered, managed or facilitated. The term 'facilitator' describes the person who initiates and plans the group, conducts the group while it is 'meeting' and manages its finishing. Facilitators need to make some plans and consider how they can fulfil the role before setting up the group in question. Chapter 2 will look at this area in more detail. Sharry (2001, p5) suggests that *the aim of the facilitator is to establish the conditions and trust in the group whereby clients can help one another and then to 'get out of the way' to allow them to do it* – although, as we will see later, the extent to which this is possible will depend on the type of group in question.

Situation	Examples of populations	Examples of settings
People functioning adequately normally but now facing some traumatic event or those who continue to be affected by a trauma experienced in the past	Survivors of physical, domestic or sexual violence	Hospital social work Women's Aid Community Mental Health Teams Voluntary agencies
	Witnesses of same	Voluntary agencies, e.g. Omagh Support and Self Help Group, London Recovers
	Facing or recovering from major surgery or debilitating or terminal illness	Hospital social work Voluntary agencies
	Ex-service personnel	Military Families Support Group SSAFA
People who themselves have been functioning adequately but who are in a close relationship with others who generate special stress for them (linked fate)	Carers, including those listed below.	
	Parents of children with physical or mental handicap	Family and childcare teams Day centre teams Barnardo's
	Partners of people with terminal, life-threatening, or debilitating conditions	Hospital social work Voluntary agencies, e.g. carers' support groups
	Partners, parents or children of people who are abusing drugs or alcohol	Mental Health Teams Drug and alcohol abuse agencies and support organisations, e.g. Al-Anon, Adfam, Alateen, Families Anonymous
	Partners or children of prisoners	NACRO Probation services Prisoners' Families and Friends Service
People experiencing or anticipating some life transition	People with a diagnosis of terminal illness	Older people team Hospital teams Hospices

Table 1.1: Who might benefit from groupwork?

Situation	Examples of populations	Examples of settings
	Recently divorced or separated people	Aquila Care Trust Divorce Recovery Workshop
	Bereaved people	Cruse Bereavement Care Hospices
	Young people	Leaving Care Teams Family and childcare teams Youth services Young offender teams
	New or young parents	NCT Barnardo's Family support services
	People being discharged from or being admitted to long-term care in hospital or residential setting	Hospital social work Prison welfare Children's residential services Leaving Care Teams
People seen by self or others as functioning below capacity	People with mental health problems	Mental Health Teams
	People with eating disorders	Mental Health Teams Family and childcare teams
	People with substance misuse problems	Drug agencies Youth Offending Teams Mental Health Teams
People who need help to overcome an ongoing specific problem	People with eating disorders People with phobias People with problems of obsessive or compulsive behaviour	Mental Health Teams Voluntary agencies
People who have lost or never fully acquired basic social, interpersonal or practical living skills	People with learning disabilities	Learning disability teams
	Ex-psychiatric patients	Mental Health Teams
	Institutionalised people	Resident settings Leaving Care Teams

Table 1.1: Continued

Situation	Examples of populations	Examples of settings
People regarded by others as having or being problems	Offenders	Probation services NACRO Youth justice agencies
	Substance misusers	Drug and alcohol agencies Mental Health Teams
	Disruptive children	Family and childcare teams Barnardo's NSPCC Youth justice agencies
	Perpetrators of abuse	Women's Aid Family and childcare teams Probation services NSPCC
People who are oppressed or disadvantaged due to their membership of a particular minority or oppressed group	People who face discrimination on the grounds of their age, colour, culture, disability, gender, religion, sexuality, etc.	Throughout statutory and voluntary agencies

Table 1.1: Continued

We can perceive the principal tasks to be fourfold, as follows:

- planning the group;
- intervening in the group;
- monitoring the group;
- maintaining the group.

We will discuss each of these in detail in later chapters.

Throughout this chapter, we have encouraged the development of your self-awareness, particularly your behaviour and responses when in a variety of groups. Earlier, we suggested that behaviour was a choice. Now, as we consider facilitation, the benefit of your reflection and consideration of your choices of behaviour will begin to have meaning. As facilitators, we cannot begin to change our behaviour so that it fits with the aims and intentions of the group until we are aware of how we might behave in the context in which we will be working. Here are two questions that we should ask ourselves.

- Do we have issues with, or experience of, the subject matter?
- Are we aware of any issues in our lives that might be re-stimulated or that we might wish to avoid?

The development of awareness is an ongoing lifelong process. To begin to facilitate effectively you need to be aware of this connection and work with it. No two groups are the same and no two methods will be exactly the same; the method and style of facilitation will *move* with the group. As a group gradually begins to take more and more responsibility for itself, the facilitation role changes. One of the most common challenges for new facilitators is to know when to intervene or interpret less, in order to allow participants to discover and understand for themselves.

In later chapters, we will be looking in more depth at facilitation and also co-facilitation. This will include planning and preparation, beginning a group, facilitation styles and intervention, working with different aspects of group process, including dealing with emotion and challenging situations, and the closing and ending of groups. We will also consider the support and supervision needs of facilitators and the choice of colleagues and consultants to work with you.

RESEARCH SUMMARY

Now consider your reflections on the groups we have discussed.

- *What are the moments or recollections of groups that stand out?*

- *Was there an element of embarrassment, risk or conflict in the situation?*

- *What worries you most about group facilitation?*

ACTIVITY *1.6*

Think now of a group that you can imagine yourself setting up in the next six months or so.

- *What user group is this to be? This could be a fairly wide group, such as 'older people', 'young offenders', 'carers', or something a little more specific, such as 'young people leaving care', 'young single parents', 'carers of young people with Asperger's syndrome'.*

- *What are their needs? It might be useful to think of Maslow's Hierarchy of Needs to help with this (if you are not familiar with this, see Trevithick, 2005b, pp92–4, or visit websites such as en.wikipedia.org/wiki/Maslow%27s_hierarchy_of_needs).*

- *How might these needs be best met through groupwork?*

COMMENT

We will use this example that you have imagined as the basis for a longer activity to which we will return on a number of occasions, as you work your way through the rest of the book.

FURTHER READING

General reading

Brown, A (1992) *Groupwork*, 3rd edition. Aldershot: Arena.

This text has an accessible discussion of the advantages and disadvantages of the groupwork method.

Doel, M and Sawdon, C (1999) *The Essential Groupworker.* London: Jessica Kingsley.

This book contains a useful chapter in which the authors discuss reasons to use and not to use groupwork.

Heron, J (1999) *The Complete Facilitator's Handbook.* London: Kogan Page.

Heron provides detailed, complex and comprehensive guidance, models and theories on the nature of facilitation and the tasks involved.

Whitaker, DS (1985) *Using Groups to Help People.* London: Routledge & Kegan Paul.

You will find here an excellent chapter on the beneficial characteristics of small helping groups.

Reading in relation to particular populations

Chesner, A (1998) *Groupwork with Learning Disabilities: Creative drama.* Milton Keynes: Speechmark Publishing.

This provides basic information and guidance on using creative drama to enhance social skills and improve self-esteem with groups of people with learning disabilities. It includes useful exercises and photocopiable activities.

Geldard, K and Geldard, D (2001) *Working with Children in Groups.* London: Palgrave Macmillan.

This is an excellent book not only in terms of working with groups of children, but in working with groups generally. There is a good combination of theory and practical advice. The final part contains four very useful programmes for working with children who have come from families where domestic violence has occurred, children with a diagnosis of attention deficit hyperactivity disorder (ADHD), children with low self-esteem and children who have difficulty with social skills. It is an essential text for anyone wishing to practise groupwork with children.

Greif, GL and Ephross, PH (2010) *Group Work with Populations at Risk*, 3rd edition. Oxford: Oxford University Press.

This is an American publication but has wide applicability. Topics include groupwork with older adults, adult survivors of child sexual abuse, people with a diagnosis of cancer, people with serious mental health problems, people living with HIV and AIDS, adolescents at risk of alcohol and drug misuse, victims of hate crime, women who have experienced abuse, children impacted by sexual abuse, and gay men, lesbians and groups for men. Some of the content may be a little advanced for beginning groupworkers, but there is much of substance in these chapters.

Hull, KB (2013) *Group Therapy Techniques with Children, Adolescents, and Adults on the Autism Spectrum: Growth and connection for all ages.* Lanham, MD: Jason Aronson.

Groupwork is not often considered as an approach for work with this service-user group due to their problems in coping with group situations. However, this text makes a strong argument for successful groupwork with the age groups indicated in the title. The sections relating to children and adolescents offer useful suggestions for groupwork with the aim of increasing the understanding of emotions, achieving better emotional control, increasing perspective taking and enhancing self-worth and awareness.

Schweitzer, P (2008) *Remembering Yesterday, Caring Today: Reminiscence in dementia care: a guide to good practice.* London: Jessica Kingsley.

This is a practical guide encompassing both group and one-to-one work, but which contains useful advice on organising a group project and planning the group, and also detailed descriptions of activities that can be used in reminiscence work.

Velasquez, MM, Maurer, GG, Crouch, C and DiClemente, CC (2011) *Group Treatment for Substance Abuse: A Stages-of-Change therapy manual.* New York: Guilford Press.

A practical manual of groupwork with substance misusers, delivered in one sequence of 29 sessions or in two sequences of 14 and 15 sessions. The manual will be of particular value to practitioners already familiar with the Stages of Change model and motivational interviewing theory and practice.

Chapter 2
Planning your group:
initial planning decisions

Introduction

We agree with Thomas and Pender (2008, cited in DeLucia-Waack and Nitza, 2013) that it is best practice for the essential design and planning of groups to take place before the first group member is contacted. Planning is the most important part of the groupwork task. You should invest at least as much time and effort in the planning of the group as actually working with it. Good planning will make a successful outcome much more likely and will reduce worry and stress as many problems will be anticipated and avoided. Decisions made about who will be involved, and when, where and how a group will work, will hugely influence its success or failure. As Corey (2004, p80) advises:

> *It is a time well spent to think about what kind of group you want and to get yourself psychologically ready. If your expectations are unclear, and if the purposes and structure of the group are vague, the members will surely engage in unnecessary floundering.*

First, who is to do the planning? The fact that the practice of groupwork is underpinned by ideas of democracy and empowerment suggests that perhaps the group members should be involved in the planning. However, how can this be if the group does not yet exist? In some cases, participants can be involved in planning from the early stages, but even this needs planning! Let us assume that you will be the person who is going to have the initial responsibility.

Planning is an activity you will be engaged in throughout your involvement in a groupwork project. Every group session will need to be planned in detail and this may only be possible as the group progresses, as you will continually need to make adjustments depending on how the group develops. Perhaps, even when you are finished, you will immediately start to plan the next group, taking into account the learning from this one. However, for now we will look only at the preliminary decisions in which you need to involve yourself. These are decisions that you will need to make before you even see a member of the group. In this chapter, we will discuss the planning process from the identification of a need that might be met by a groupwork project, through such considerations as group size, mix, frequency and duration, to thinking about how you might ensure you obtain the essential support of your agency and colleagues.

What preliminary decisions do you have to make in planning your group?

At the end of each of the relevant chapters, we will provide you with a pro forma that you can use to plan your group. We will ask you to use this to plan the imaginary group you identified at the end of Chapter 1. However, you will also be able to piece the parts of the pro forma together and this will be of use to you when you come to plan a group for real. The pro forma follows the structure of the chapters in the book.

In Figure 2.1 is a tool showing the stages for identifying, preparing, planning and organising a task, in this case a groupwork project. Writing down the *directional phases* can often prompt tough questions and can be very useful for making a case or rationale for the work, both for you and for colleagues and other agencies involved.

Why meet as a group?

Is there a need to be met? Whose needs are we meeting if we form a group? There are the fundamental questions. Social work students are required to demonstrate practice skills and knowledge in working with groups in order to qualify. Immediately, we can identify a *student* need for a group. Other practitioners may prefer groupwork as a way of working

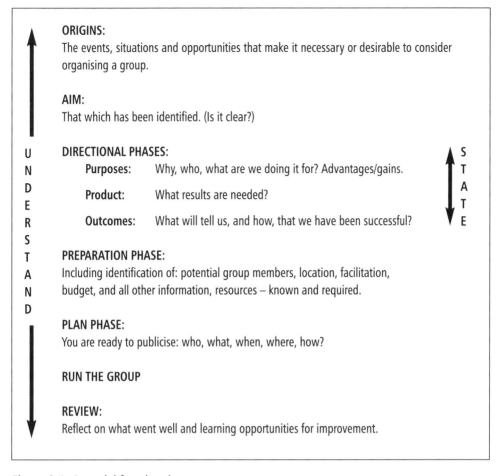

ORIGINS:
The events, situations and opportunities that make it necessary or desirable to consider organising a group.

AIM:
That which has been identified. (Is it clear?)

DIRECTIONAL PHASES:

Purposes: Why, who, what are we doing it for? Advantages/gains.

Product: What results are needed?

Outcomes: What will tell us, and how, that we have been successful?

PREPARATION PHASE:
Including identification of: potential group members, location, facilitation, budget, and all other information, resources – known and required.

PLAN PHASE:
You are ready to publicise: who, what, when, where, how?

RUN THE GROUP

REVIEW:
Reflect on what went well and learning opportunities for improvement.

Figure 2.1 A model for planning

with people, perhaps disliking the intimacy of one-to-one work. We wrote earlier of the potential for personal prestige that arises from a successful group project and that is perhaps more difficult to obtain through individual work. Agencies may be persuaded that groupwork is a cost-effective way of working and apply pressure on, or even require, staff to work in this way. Nevertheless, while other reasons can be both important and legitimate, the primary focus for groupworkers must be the identification of unmet service user need.

ACTIVITY **2.1**

Thinking about the group you identified at the end of the last chapter, write down your answers to the following questions.

- *What needs does this group of people usually have that possibly are not being met?*

- *For which of these needs might groupwork be particularly suitable and why?*

Some beginning groupworkers make the mistake of identifying a category of people to work with as a group, rather than identifying a need to be met. A need is quite different from a category. For example, we may think it would be a good idea to set up a group for a category – older people in residential care, young single parents – but intervention in people's lives can only be justified if there is a need to be met – the need for social contact, the need to develop skills in childcare. Has your answer met this requirement?

Is this need shared by a number of people who could potentially benefit from being in a group?

Are there enough people in your area who share this problem to form a group? You may, for example, be working in the social work department of a general hospital and come to realise that a number of patients have experienced loss and have a need for support and sharing. However, are they in sufficient numbers to make up a group? Will they still be there by the time you are ready to start and are you reasonably sure that a sufficient number of them would be interested in attending?

Is a group the most appropriate way of meeting this need?

Is it possible that another method of intervention, perhaps one-to-one work or family therapy, would be more fitting or more likely to be effective? In the particular setting in which you are working, there will already be a body of research that can help you with this question, and to which you should refer, or it may be possible to learn from the experience of other workers.

Students often ask 'What sort of a groupwork project could I run in my current placement with this service-user group?' The question usually arises because a student is under pressure to run a group to satisfy the requirements of his or her practice teacher or social work programme to produce evidence of competence in running a group. If the student's motivation to deliver a groupwork programme arises from his or her desire to satisfy a personal need to complete a placement successfully, rather than any need existing in the service-user population, then he or she is starting in the wrong place. Let us reiterate this most important point: the first question must always be 'What unmet need is there here that could be met effectively by a group?'

It is not possible for us to give specific guidance here on the needs of different groups. This is far too huge since needs can vary significantly even within any one group. Geldard and Geldard's (2001) text on working with children in groups illustrates the problem. They give the example of children who have been brought up in families against a background of violence. They show that the needs of such children will vary with their age. Children from violent families from age seven to nine may have the following needs:

- to reconstruct their beliefs around male–female relationships;

- to learn alternative ways of responding to others in conflict situations;

- to understand that the rules and consequences at home cannot be generalised into wider society.

Children who are aged from nine to adolescence, on the other hand, may have different needs:

- to deal with the stigmatisation of coming from a violent family;
- to develop different social skills in relating to peers of the opposite sex;
- to develop a healthy self-concept that is not based on family stereotypes.

The point being made here is that, in determining these children's needs, groupworkers need to take into consideration the children's experiences, psychological state and developmental stage and the interaction among these three factors. Of course, any one of the needs identified above could provide the basis for a group. Imagine now, though, the range of needs we may identify when we come to think about other situations and other service users – parents, young people, adults and older people, and people with physical disabilities, learning disabilities, mental health problems, and drug and alcohol problems.

However, and on perhaps a more positive note, there nearly always are opportunities for useful and helpful groupwork intervention in a particular context and at a particular time (see Table 1.1, pages 17–19, for examples of categories of people for whom groupwork may be helpful). The skill lies in identifying the need and thinking through how it will be met, but there is no short cut. Engaging the services users themselves in discussion, talking and seeking the advice of your practice teacher and her or his colleagues will be helpful. You must carefully assess the needs of the individuals for whom you are hoping to provide a service. A search of the literature, both groupwork and in respect of the service-user group itself, will help you in understanding the characteristics of this group in a more general sense. You will also be able to find examples of groups that have proved successful in the past.

What is to be the aim of the group?

Having decided on an unmet need or needs that can be met by groupwork and that is/are shared by enough people, you should now be able to encapsulate the purpose of the group in a clearly stated aim or set of aims. In deciding on the expressed aims of the group, you should bear a number of things in mind. Initially, it is useful to set aims that are rather general. These may be refined later. Here is an example from Phillips (2006, p29). It is taken from a group for young women attending a community centre. In this case, it was possible and appropriate to establish the aims in discussion with the members at an initial meeting of the group. The aims were:

- *to highlight the main issues and concerns young women face today;*
- *to offer one-to-one advice and support;*
- *to improve young women's awareness and understanding of sexual discrimination.*

Note how each aim starts with the word 'to'.

Benson shows how it is very useful to have clear aims or goals.

- *Goals help to motivate people, both workers and members. They state a position at which we wish to arrive.*

- *They help avoid or resolve conflict.*

- *They give us a means of judging how successful we have been.*

- *Goals can provide us with ideas about how to get to where we want to be. Once we are clear about what we want to achieve we can then make decisions about how we will achieve it.*

(2001, p18)

In formulating your aims it may be helpful for you to bear in mind the SMART acronym.

- **S**pecific – you should be specific about what you aim to achieve.

- **M**easurable – you should be able to measure whether you have achieved your aims.

- **A**chievable – ensure that the aims you set are achievable and attainable. For example, are they within the abilities of the group members? Do not be overly ambitious. Remember the needs that the group members have may be highly complex, and may have arisen over a considerable period. Do not expect that difficulties that have taken a long time to come about will be easily resolved. They also may be functional in some way for the person or for someone else. A young person who repeatedly has problems in school or who is frequently before the courts is likely to have a number of other problems – with learning, with relationships, or with drugs perhaps – but this situation may also be functional for parents, who may prefer to see a problem as lying with the young person rather than confront problems in their own relationship.

- **R**elevant – relevant to the agency function; relevant to the needs of the service users. Another point is that, at least in the early stages of a group, the stated aims may not be exactly the same as those of the members.

- **T**ime/Timely/Tangible – Time: within what timescale do you want to achieve the aim? Timely: you need to think about whether this is the right time to set up the group. Tangible: how might people experience the difference a group might make?

RESEARCH SUMMARY

Manktelow and Lindsay (2003) conducted an evaluation of a family support team that ran a range of Sure Start services for parents (mostly mothers) in the team catchment area. In addition to services for children, such as crèches and play schools, a number of groupwork services were provided for the parents. The latter included a breastfeeding support group, a group providing learning on issues regarding parenting toddlers, a baby massage group, a young parents' programme, a behaviour management programme and adult education programmes, in addition to a number of programmes simply providing support and social opportunities. In the evaluation of the services, it was discovered that a significant number of parents had been receiving a range of services for some time and it transpired that they were accessing services mainly for the incidental social and support benefits, rather than necessarily to avail themselves of the benefits suggested by the groups' stated aims.

There is nothing wrong with the aims of the members being different from those of the facilitators, so long as these are complementary. However, we should also be aware that this will not always be the case. Frequently, the aims of the facilitators and the members will come closer together as the group develops. What is important is that initially there is enough common ground between the purpose of the agency and the purposes of the members in taking part.

Example
A fully SMART example might be:

> *to facilitate carers of adult dependants in increasing their use of respite care before the end of the year.*

ACTIVITY 2.2

Thinking again about the group you identified earlier, write down an overall aim.

COMMENT

Does your aim start with 'to'? Does it satisfy the SMART criteria?

How are the group aims and objectives to be met?

Having decided what needs the service users have that may be met through groupwork, and having formulated the aims of the group, you should have some ideas about what the group will do in order to achieve these and thus what sort of group it will be. What follows are some of the types of groups that commonly take place. These are set out as if there are set types of groups and, of course, this is not necessarily the case. Some groups will be a mixture of:

- support and discussion groups;
- skill-development groups – social skills, parenting skills, literacy;
- therapeutic groups – bereavement, trauma, psychodynamic, gestalt, cognitive, behavioural;
- action groups – where the group is set up to achieve some desired change outside the group, for example age concern, child poverty, improved housing, community issues;
- activity groups – walking, cookery, reading;
- self-help groups – community, women's groups.

These categories soon suggest the activities that will take place during the life of the group and we will look at these in more detail in Chapter 6.

How is the group to be structured?

The structure of the group is very important as it has an impact on how the group will run and on the outcomes. At this stage in our planning, we are able to get into more detail about the structure of the group. This includes deciding on the composition of the group, its size, its frequency and length, and other practical issues, such as where and when it will meet. Different types of groups call for different decisions at this stage. In many cases the decisions we arrive at will carry both advantages and disadvantages. Douglas (1995) argues that these factors are interrelated, so that changes in one characteristic will inevitably affect another. For example, a group that has open membership may become larger – the size of the group will determine where it can take place – the location of the venue will have an impact on the balance of the people able to attend.

Douglas (1995) lists 11 factors, while Doel and Sawdon (1999) list 12 variables, between them identifying a total of 17 different aspects to be taken into account. Each of these presents us with a continuum with opposites at either end. For example, in terms of length, a group can run for either a long or a short period; each has advantages and disadvantages. Some of these factors we will deal with shortly. Not all the structural aspects are within the control of the worker: some will be predetermined. If we decide to work with a pre-existing group, perhaps the residents of a hostel or a group of young people who go round together, we may not have control over the size of the group. Nevertheless, we should be aware of what the implications of these 'givens' are, so that potential difficulties can be avoided.

Size

The size of the group will have an impact on how it is experienced, both by the members and by the leaders, so the optimum size will depend on the type of group being planned. A group that has the aim of facilitating members in expressing their feelings needs to be sufficiently small for the members to feel safe enough, but a larger group, set up to tackle a shared problem, may come up with a greater number of solutions. Most groupworkers seem to find that, for groups based on open discussion, the optimum number of members is from six to eight. Activity-based groups, where some of the time is spent in activities in sub-groups, can be rather larger, say 12 or more. Hawkins and Alden (1981, cited in Whitaker, 1985) found that, in groups of four or fewer, norms tended to become established that worked against the therapeutic process.

Benson (2001) suggests the variables shown in Table 2.1. Additionally, Brown (1992) suggests those shown in Table 2.2.

Remember, most groups experience a certain amount of drop-out. If the optimum number in your group is eight, you will probably need to recruit ten members to allow for drop-out.

Time

Rapin and Crowell (2013) consider time as a resource of which you must take account. In addition to how often the group will meet and for how long, which we discuss below, you also need to consider the appropriateness of your timing of the group. Will you and any others involved be able to commit yourselves to the time, not just in terms of workload but in terms of family and holiday commitments? Are times appropriate for members, for example taking into account school times for groups containing pupils or parents with childcare responsibilities? No one would consider planning a group to run on a Sunday morning, but what about a Friday afternoon and problems that this might cause for Muslim members?

	As group gets smaller
Support	increases
Intimacy	increases
Satisfaction	increases
Opportunities for participation	increase
Consensus	increases
Personal recognition	increases
Emergence of subgroups	decreases
Reliance on facilitator	decreases
Need for formal procedures and rules	decreases
Length of time to solve problems	decreases
Number of personal relationships	decreases
Ability to tackle more complex problems	decreases
Creativity	decreases

Table 2.1: Variables based on group size, according to Benson (2001)

	As group gets smaller
Participation of the more reticent members	increases
Physical freedom (e.g. space, time)	increases
Psychological freedom (opportunity to rest, hide, identify with others)	decreases
Emergence of specific roles	decreases
Participation of active/talkative members	decreases

Table 2.2: Variables based on group size, according to Brown (1992)

Frequency

The frequency of meetings will be determined by the benefits you hope for the group and the character of the people in the group. The factor that comes into play here is the ratio of time spent in the group to that spent elsewhere. Whitaker (1985) suggests that the frequency of group meetings influences the group experience in three ways.

- **Intensity** – The more frequently a group meets, the more intense the experience is likely to be. For some groups we may wish the experience to be intense and, for others, we may not; we may feel that too much intensity may be overwhelming or simply unnecessary.

- **Importance** – Groups that meet more frequently and/or for longer are likely to assume greater importance in the members' lives. This may be desirable, for example in the case of people with physical disabilities who may need a reference group, or undesirable, for example where the aim is to encourage independence.

- **Continuity** – Groups that meet less frequently tend to lose any sense of continuity. Each session is like starting over. Again, this may not be undesirable, but needs to be borne in mind, for example by making sure that each session has its own focus.

Duration

How long will the group exist? Once more, this will depend on the purpose of the group. Short-term groups of five or six sessions are useful for certain specific purposes, for example preparing people to join or leave an institution, or providing information on health issues or childcare. Other groups, aimed at therapeutic experiences, need time for necessary trust-building to take place. Some groups are set up with a timescale of some months; others are planned to keep going for as long as the need exists, without any end date in mind.

Constancy of membership

Is membership to be closed or open? Closed groups start and finish with the same members, whereas the membership of an open group changes as people join and leave. There are pros and cons with both. Very rapid turnover of membership, with members dropping out and being replaced, affects the level of intimacy that can be achieved. This may be unavoidable with groups based on an ever-changing population, such as in a hospital ward, but it will affect the type of group possible. Solutions include setting up the group with a short lifespan or organising a group where constancy of membership or attendance is not vital to the work of the group. Another possibility is to organise the group to have set intake periods when the membership is reopened for a short period. Some groups that run to a set programme organise the content on a modular basis, so that people join at the beginning of modules.

Composition

ACTIVITY 2.3

You are working in a mental health fieldwork team. You have decided to run a group for the parents of young people with eating disorders. The aim of the group is to provide support and the opportunity to exchange ideas about how to cope with the situation. You have decided that the optimum number for the group is between eight and ten. You have advertised the group in your team and have had the following referrals.

Janet – 40, with two children, the elder of whom, May, aged 20, is bulimic. Janet is a sales assistant. Janet's partner Gail died a few weeks ago in a car accident. Although it was not her fault, Janet was driving and is still feeling very distressed and responsible for the death. She is very worried about May's health and is keen to learn ways to control her bulimia.

Gertrude – 39, single parent with four children. Godfrey, the eldest, has anorexia nervosa and is very withdrawn. Gertrude is on state benefits and finds it difficult to manage financially. She is socially isolated and requires a lot of support. She is very enthusiastic about the prospect of a group.

Sally – 37, married with one child, Suzy, who is anorexic. Sally is a bank official and her husband is an independent financial adviser. His work takes him away from home a lot.

Jane – the 72-year-old widowed grandmother of Emma, 18, who is bulimic. Emma moved to her grandmother's following a row with her parents. Jane suffers from back pain and is worried about how she will get to the group, but her daughter has offered to take her.

Alice – 49, with two teenage girls, of whom the younger, Rachel, aged 15, is anorexic. Alice is married to Philip, a taxi driver. Alice is highly anxious and is unable to stop talking when her social worker visits the home. She is also often very tearful when discussing problems with Rachel. She is very keen to join the group.

Philip – 44, Alice's husband. He is very concerned about Rachel and would like to attend the group. He is keen on the idea of a group and he says that it would be helpful to Alice if he went also. Unfortunately, he can only attend two weeks in every three due to his work pattern.

Georgina – 34, a single parent with one daughter, Rose, who is 16 and anorexic. Georgina is on state benefits.

Surrinder – 55, a Sikh woman, who is married with three children. Her husband Karim is an assembler in a factory. The middle daughter, Amrit, is anorexic.

Alex – 54, married to Ron, with one daughter, Kim. Alex and Ron run a market stall. Kim suffers from obsessive-compulsive disorder, which results in a great deal of tension and difficulty around eating.

Mike – 44, and divorced. His daughter, Gloria, aged 19, lives with him and suffers from bulimia. Mike gets upset about the bulimia and would be glad to have some people to talk to about it.

Debosa – 39, a black Nigerian woman with two children. Her daughter, Linda, is 16 and is anorexic. Debosa lives with her partner, James, who also has two children from a previous relationship. Both are on state benefits.

Anne – 53, married with three children, the youngest of whom is anorexic. Anne is a hairdresser and her husband is a car mechanic. Her social worker says that, although she is only lukewarm, she would benefit greatly from attending.

You need to select eight, nine or ten from these twelve to make up the group membership. Which two, three or four are you going to leave out (perhaps until the next time)? Make a note of your decisions and the reasons for them. We will return to this after the next paragraph.

COMMENT

We will discuss shortly some different factors in group composition to be taken into consideration. As we do, we will refer back to the scenario in Activity 2.3 when this is relevant.

The extent to which you will have the power to decide on the actual composition of a group will vary considerably from situation to situation. As Whitaker (1985) suggests, there will be different routes for defining the actual membership. Sometimes, there will be no choice, such as when the group is to be formed by all the people in a group home, or by people who have been ordered to attend by a court.

Other groups might be formed by open invitation to a potential population of participants, for example the parents in a particular area of children with learning disabilities. In other circumstances you may be able to choose the members from a larger list. However, in our experience, this is comparatively rare in social work. It is often more a matter of working with the people with whom one is working already or who have been referred by colleagues. In these circumstances numbers may not be sufficiently large for selection to be an issue. However, we do need to avoid compositions that will result in the group becoming unworkable.

Even when we do not have much power to select, it is important for us to know how the composition of the group will influence its behaviour. We will need to consider this also in other decisions we make about the structure of the group, bearing in mind the point about the interrelatedness of these different factors made by Douglas (1995) and mentioned earlier. We will also need to consider these influences once the group is running and make our plans accordingly.

- **Homogeneity/heterogeneity** – Much has been written on the topic of homogeneity and heterogeneity, that is, the extent to which a group is made up of people with similar characteristics (homogeneous) or who differ considerably (heterogeneous). Brown (1992, p47), arguing that this is the key decision in group composition, cites Redl's (1951) *Law of Optimum Distance*, which states that groups should be *homogeneous enough to ensure stability and heterogeneous enough to ensure vitality*. Whitaker (2001) suggests that groups work best if they are homogeneous in respect of level of vulnerability and heterogeneous in respect of preferred defences.

RESEARCH SUMMARY

Research by Bertcher and Marple (1977, cited in Brown, 1992) suggests that an effective approach is to construct membership on the basis of homogeneity of descriptive attributes – that is, factual descriptions such as age, gender, class, ethnicity, and so on, and on the basis of heterogeneity of behavioural attributes, such as personality, attitudes and lifestyles. The point here is that similarity in terms of age, gender, race and class is likely to foster cohesiveness, while a mix of people with different behavioural attributes is likely to result in a group that is more interesting and dynamic.

Bertcher and Marple's research puts a different complexion on our example. Jane is much older than the others are, Debosa and Surrinder are ethnically different from the others, and Sally seems to be removed from the others in terms of class. Should you exclude any or all of these?

- **Isolation** – It is useful to avoid compositions that isolate one individual within the group (e.g. one black or Asian member in a group that is otherwise white; one man in a group that is otherwise female).

REFLECTION POINT

So, what should we do about the two men in the group? Here is a dilemma. Philip and Alice are the only couple. Is it a good idea to have a sole couple in the group? But then, if Philip is not in the group, the only other man, Mike, will be on his own. What do you think we should do? Make a list of the pros and cons; then write down your decision and the reasons for it.

- **Gender** – Men and women differ considerably in both their attitudes and behaviour in groups and this can be a major factor in how the group is conducted. In some circumstances the purpose of the group may dictate that it should be of single gender.

RESEARCH SUMMARY

In a study of decision-making, the Affirmative Action Agency (1995) found that, in mixed-gender committees, men take up between 58 and 86 per cent of speaking time, well in excess of their level of representation. The same study found that, while 81 per cent of men reported being satisfied with their contribution to meetings, only 61 per cent of women did so, and similarly that 62 per cent of women compared to 82 per cent of men felt that they were able to say what they wanted to say.

Aries (1976) conducted a number of observations of both mixed and single-gender groups. She reported a number of differences in differently constructed groups that affected the thematic content and social interaction. Women talked more often to males than to females in mixed groups. Men were more likely, in either mixed or single groups, to initiate conversation and to address the group as a whole. Women were more likely to express direct concern around interpersonal issues, whereas men tended to do so indirectly, utilising metaphors and stories. Men talked more about emotions in mixed groups than in single-gender groups. Aries concluded that mixed groups benefit men by allowing more variation in their interpersonal style, whereas women in mixed groups were restricted in interpersonal style.

A study by Smith-Lovin and Brody (1989) found that men in groups tend to yield to interruptions from other men but not from women, whereas women yield equally to interruptions from either gender.

Research by Doherty and Enders (1993) suggests that, while mixed groups can be helpful in the development of intimate heterosexual relationships, women who have been victimised by males fare better in single-gender groups. Women who have been subjected to sexual or domestic violence need the opportunity to discuss their experiences and feelings in a single-gender group. Hodgins et al. (1997), summarising research into single-gender and mixed groups for substance misusers, argue that, because men and women have different needs and characteristics in relation to substance misuse, they require single-gender treatment groups.

Brown (1992) refers to evidence that suggests that all-female groups give more attention to issues of emotions and relationships, while all-male groups tend to be more competitive and status-oriented. This, he suggests, has important implications when we come to constructing mixed-gender groups. Generally speaking, in mixed groups the women often 'accommodate' the men by facilitating their capacity to express their feelings. However, this is without any obvious equivalent benefit to them. Consequently, Brown suggests that mixed groups where at least half the members are female are likely to be more successful, as an ethos akin to an all-female group is more likely to prevail.

All-male groups are also appropriate, frequently for 'negative' reasons – that is, as the perpetrators of violence – but also for positive reasons, such as the development of fathering skills, awareness or the expression of feelings.

- **Age** – The older the profile of the group, the more likely it is to be comfortable with a range of ages. A range of ten or twenty years is likely to be acceptable in a group of mature adults, whereas even two or three years can be too much for a group of teenagers.

REFLECTION POINT

Alice is much older than the others. Does this matter? Anne and Alex are in their fifties. At this age, this sort of gap is not likely to make a big difference in this type of group.

- **Ethnicity** – Some of the issues discussed in relation to gender also apply to ethnicity. It may be appropriate to have an all-black group, for purposes of affirmation or to be able to discuss issues of racism and oppression in a safe environment. Equally, it may be important to bring different ethnicities together so that they can learn of each other's experiences. The question of mixed groups, however, is a little more complicated than it is for mixed gender, simply because of the demographics involved. Since black people are in the minority in the population, they are also likely to be in the minority in the group. This may create disadvantages for them, especially if they are perceived by the white members primarily as being black, rather than people with whom they have needs in common. To some extent, the disadvantages can be overcome, for example by ensuring that one of the facilitators is black. If the group is frequently repeated, it may be possible to run a more balanced group when sufficient members of both populations become available. A word of caution is needed here, however, and it applies equally to other minority situations. We need to be careful that we are not denying a service to someone in order to prevent them being in a minority situation. It would not be acceptable to delay someone's acceptance into a group if that in itself was disadvantageous.

Brown (1992) also makes a valid point about ethnicity. For a group that is dealing with issues of racism, ethnic differences between black people may not be as important as their common experience of oppression, but for other groups cultural differences within ethnic minority populations need to be considered and taken into account.

COMMENT

In our example we have two people from ethnic minorities – Debosa and Surrinder. They might not feel so isolated in the group together, as they would if they were on their own. However, although they could both be considered as black people, they might not agree and, being from different ethnic groups, may not be able to support each other all that much. Maybe we should discuss this with them, tell them how the group is being constructed and get their views on how they feel about participating in the group.

- **Exclusions** – It is important to remember that people who have had a traumatic experience, even if it happened years ago, are likely to need the opportunity to talk it through in the safety and privacy of a one-to-one relationship before they feel strong enough to cope with group discussion on the topic. In the case study below, the women had not yet reached a stage where they could listen to the traumatic experiences of others, still less discuss their own. It was beyond their frontier.

CASE STUDY

A mental health social worker decided to run a group for a number of survivors of childhood sexual abuse and constructed the group out of a combination of service users with whom she had been working on a one-to-one basis and others who were referred by colleagues. There appeared to be an obvious need for these women to come together to reduce feelings of isolation and misplaced guilt and to support each other. The first session went well but, during the second session, two of the women became very distressed and did not return to the group. The group facilitator visited them to find out why they had stopped coming. Both women told her that they had never discussed their experiences in any detail before and found it very upsetting to hear others do so.

Other people may need to be excluded to avoid them preventing progress for others in the group or even harming others in the group. This includes people who are very disorganised or disruptive, so that they have a limited capacity to listen to others, even for a short period of time. At the extreme end of the spectrum are people who have so little control over themselves that they are assessed as presenting a risk of violence to other members or the facilitators. As Corey (2004) suggests, the presence of some people can make it difficult to achieve cohesion in the group, for example people who have an overwhelming need to monopolise or dominate, or who are very hostile or aggressive. Screening people out of the group is not to be taken lightly and you may well need to meet them face to face to ensure that a decision to exclude them is not oppressive. We will discuss preliminary interviews with potential group members in Chapter 4. However, before deciding to exclude someone from a group there is a final question we must ask ourselves. Is there any way in which the plan for the group might be altered to allow for this person to be included? It may be, for example, that the person could cope satisfactorily with a group with a high level of activity, rather than one based on discussion.

But, then again, we have to take into account the benefit for the whole group and not just one individual. On the other hand, a completely different group might be able to meet this individual's need, so someone with a severe substance misuse problem might not be appropriate to include in a personal growth group, at this stage, but benefit well from a specialist group for people with a similar problem.

ACTIVITY 2.4

Thinking back over your life, do you remember an occasion on which you were excluded from a group? How did that feel?

COMMENT

Being excluded nearly always feels bad and can be very hurtful, even damaging. We need to approach the decision to exclude someone with great care. Such a decision can only be justified on the grounds that it will be potentially harmful to either themselves or others if they are not excluded.

ACTIVITY 2.5

Think about the circumstances in which it might be appropriate to exclude someone from a group. Write these down under two headings: 'Exclude to avoid harm to the person' and 'Exclude to avoid harm to others'.

COMMENT

A group may not be an appropriate method of helping for some individuals. These include people in an acute stage of crisis and people who are very vulnerable. Some people may have what Whitaker (2001) refers to as a preoccupying concern (p27) that may need to be taken into account. For example, someone who is preoccupied with a recent bereavement may not be able to participate in a group geared towards helping people maximise state benefits, or a homeless person may not be able to focus on anything other than where he or she will sleep tonight. For others, the aims of the group may be way beyond what they are capable of achieving or dealing with, either at this time or in the future – in Whitaker's terms, beyond their personal frontier (p28).

Returning to our example in Activity 2.3, we need to think about both Janet and Alice. Janet has recently had a very traumatic experience and is still very distressed. Although the trauma is not related to the purpose of the group, she is unlikely to be able to engage with the discussion at this stage. Her *preoccupying concerns* (Whitaker, 2001, p27) are likely to result in the group being of limited benefit to her. Alice seems very vulnerable and to have significant emotional needs. Will her compulsion to have these needs satisfied prevent the needs of others in the group being met?

There is no right answer to how the group in Activity 2.3 should be constructed. However, we will see in Chapter 4 that it is good practice to see potential members prior to the group starting and we would use this to explore the issues raised above, before coming to a decision.

Co-facilitation

We will discuss facilitation and co-facilitation in detail in Chapter 3, but make mention here as it is another of the decisions to be made in the preliminary planning. There are a number of advantages and also some potential problems in co-working a group. We have mentioned above the possibility of ensuring that one leader is black where the group is mixed. Equally, there are obvious advantages in having a mix in the gender of the facilitators in working with mixed-gender groups or indeed when working with perpetrator groups. However, we need to consider whether having more than one facilitator will swamp the group and inhibit the members. Again, the optimum ratio of members to facilitators will depend on the group purpose. With very small groups, it would not usually be appropriate to have more than one facilitator, while for much larger groups three or even four might be useful, especially where the group is to be activity-based, perhaps involving some physical risk. For service users who may have issues with authority, Whitaker (1985) suggests that discussion groups should not have more than two facilitators due to fears among the members about being criticised by, or subject to the disapproval of, the facilitators.

CASE STUDY

An organisation was running groups for young people thought of as being at risk of offending, drug abuse, education drop-out and other problems. The groups aimed to get the young people to confront what was wrong in their lives and so commit to change. Typically, in group sessions there would be as many facilitators as young people. When asked why this was, one of the facilitators explained that it was so that, if a young person became disruptive, there would be a facilitator available to remove the young person from the group and work with them individually.

COMMENT

We are not in a position to comment on how effective these groups may have been in achieving their stated aims. However, we wonder what the impact of having so many facilitators was on the group as a whole and on the group process (see Chapter 5). Would this example meet our earlier definition of groupwork as a method of social work that aims, through purposeful group experiences, to help individuals and groups to meet individual and group need? We will return to this topic in Chapter 6.

Venue

This decision is also of critical importance. The choice of venue will determine the eventual membership of the group, as some venues will be more comfortable for some group members than others. Often, the choice of venue seems obvious and it can boil down to what is available or what is free.

39

> ### RESEARCH SUMMARY
>
> *Lindsay and Quinn (2001) conducted an evaluation of a groupwork project run by probation staff in Belfast for young men with a risk or a record of sectarian violence, either as perpetrators or victims. The group aimed to develop their awareness of their attitudes, beliefs and prejudices through reflecting on their own lives and the experience of others. Care was taken to ensure an even balance of Catholics and Protestants, but very quickly attendance by the Catholic membership dropped to the extent that this balance (and the group) was significantly compromised. Although the workers had chosen the venue with close attention to its neutrality, the study found that a significant factor in the dropped membership was the fact that the Catholic members did not perceive it as such.*

Doel and Sawdon (1999) cite Otway (1989, p213) in their list of advantages of a venue for a particular art therapy group. This provides a useful guide to some of the issues.

1. *It was local.*

2. *It was not attached to a social services office, so possibly avoiding the stigma that can accompany a client of social services.*

3. *There was a separate room for a crèche on a different floor.*

4. *Refreshment facilities and toilets were close by.*

5. *Materials and equipment could be locked away when not in use by the group.*

6. *The room was free on the day we had set aside.*

We have now discussed many of the different factors we need to take into account in arriving at our initial plan and the influence these have on the type of group we will run. Douglas (2000, p25) refers to these factors as *constraints* in the sense that they can make a difference to whether the group will run as intended. However, before leaving this section, we wish to include a final point from Douglas. It is that very few of the constraints we have considered above are immovable. Douglas (2000, p35) argues that the basic requirements for dealing with them are as follows:

> *First, realise that they exist; second, realise their likely effects; and third, work out how best they can be set aside or more effectively used as positive rather than negative influences.*

What do I need to do to obtain the consent and support of the agency and colleagues?

Having completed the preliminary planning for your group, the next step is to seek permission from your agency to get started with setting the group up. This may not be as straightforward as you may think. Your groupwork project is doomed to failure if you do not have the support of your team and your colleagues. This is not something that will come to you automatically, no matter how good your idea might be.

Two newly qualified social workers, Shakila and Brian, working in a family and childcare team, shared their experience of working with women with children, who seemed to be very isolated during the daytime. They thought that the women would benefit from the support and company of other women who were in a similar position and that, if successful, the group could eventually run itself. They decided to discuss the idea of a group with their team leader and were surprised not to get much support. The team leader grudgingly gave them permission to go ahead, but explained that they would have to run the group in their own time and the funding would have to come from the women. They decided to go ahead with this, even though it would mean that they would have to make up the time spent on the group by working in the evenings. They then raised the idea at a team meeting and asked if team members could let them have the names of anyone who might benefit from the group. Everyone seemed quite keen but, after a week, they still had not received any names from colleagues.

Having read this case study, what do you think was going on? What issues may there have been for the line manager? Why might colleagues not have made referrals?

The situation above is not untypical and gives some idea of the issues of which we must be aware. We need to think separately about line managers and colleagues, as their concerns and interests might be quite different. Yet, we need to have the support of both. From the line managers we need permission to set up the group and also the resources to do so: staff time, materials and, most importantly, money. From our colleagues we may need referrals to the group, but also we need their support and cooperation, so that, for example, they will be flexible about rearranging tasks, times, and so on, to allow us to do the job.

Obtaining the support of the line manager

Before taking your project to your line manager, it is important to think through some managerial considerations.

- **Agency aim and purpose** – Probably the most significant consideration is how much your proposal is in keeping with the aims and objectives of the agency. Your line manager will not support you in the project if your proposal is not in keeping with the purpose and function of the agency, nor if you do not appear to have the skills, nor if the service user would not benefit from groupwork.

- **Organisational boundaries** – Your agency will have some boundary with the outside world. Is it a balloon or a tea bag?

Balloons: Some agencies are like balloons and the boundary is very obvious. The users of agencies' services are clearly defined. Hospitals only work with patients or their relatives. A manager in such an agency may not be happy about staff time and resources being spent on people who are not service users of the agency. Sometimes the agency is working within an institution, perhaps a prison or residential setting, where the demands of the group may conflict with the demands of the institution, for example concerning when the group members are available and for how long, either for each session or for the life of the group.

Teabags: Other agencies are more like tea bags, the boundaries between them and the outside world being less distinct. Agencies with a high level of involvement with the local community can be like this, or those providing preventative services, for example drug agencies, or family support and health promotion agencies.

One thing that all agencies have in common is the need to protect their reputation. This may be a matter of greater concern to the line manager than to the worker.

CASE STUDY

A group of probation officers set up a groupwork project, which involved taking a group of young offenders into the countryside for a short residential period, where they could combine outdoor pursuits with cognitive behavioural exercises. In the middle of the night, a number of the young people left the hostel through their bedroom window and went joyriding in a neighbour's car. They returned without the probation staff being aware of their absence until the police arrived later that morning. Although the group projects continued, the line manager refused permission to have further residential experiences.

In this example, the manager was concerned not only about the joyriding but the effect it had on the reputation of the agency in the local community.

- **Resources** – Managers will think in terms of a number of different resources, not only staff time and cash, but also use of materials, equipment and accommodation. Cost-effectiveness will be a major consideration and it will be helpful if you have done your homework in terms of whether this is going to offer value for money.

- **Communication** – All agencies have policies about communication with other staff about service users. This can vary tremendously. Some Women's Aid groups, for example, communicate on a need-to-know basis only, whereas in child protection policy attempts to ensure that everyone is kept well informed. You will need to decide whether necessary issues of confidentiality in your group sit easily with agency policy.

- **Workloads** – Related to the discussion above is the issue of workloads. This will not usually be a problem where you are proposing to work only with the service users on your own caseload. However, when you are proposing to work across staff workloads, you need to know if this is likely to cause a problem in the allocation of work. Try to anticipate the concerns of the line manager and take some action to remedy these, for example by offering to run the group as a pilot project, by suggesting systems of communication, and by coming up with a proposal that causes as little disruption to existing working patterns as possible.

Obtaining the support of colleagues

Colleagues may share some of the concerns of managers, and for the same reasons, or they may be worried about the same areas for reasons of their own. Is your proposal going to result in different working patterns? Will staff be kept fully informed about the people they refer? They may also have other professional concerns. Colleagues may not agree that groupwork offers benefits for the service users, believing it to be potentially harmful. Unfortunately, there may also be some negative reasons. They may want to keep their service users to themselves. They may not want to expose their previous work with the service user, or they may be jealous and resentful of you for having come up with the idea for this project. All of these are issues of which you need to be aware and deal with in some way.

One of the most successful strategies with colleagues is to get their concerns and negative attitudes out into the open. Make sure that you provide as much information as possible but try not to come across as being too clever and full of yourself. Positively invite comments and feedback on your proposals. Get them to express their fears. Help them to identify the ways in which things will change (if at all) and to be realistic and objective about the actual impact that this will have for them professionally and personally. Remember to express your general interest rather than argue for the outcome you are seeking, for example 'I am interested in making positive contact with teenage drug users on the housing estate', rather than 'I want to set up a group for teenage drug users.' Be prepared to compromise. Show them that you are prepared to discuss things openly and without being precious or defensive. It is when negative attitudes are underground that things become problematic. Referrals are never made; the room you booked ends up full of furniture; the video or DVD player you were going to use is being used elsewhere; or the members of your group decide that it is not such a good idea (and, oddly, you have heard the same objections expressed in the staff room).

Group Planner

We now introduce a useful tool for planning a groupwork project. We will bring in additional parts of the Group Planner as we go through the relevant chapters of the book. You will find them at the ends of Chapters 3, 6 and 9. You may want to put the parts together later, so that you can have a comprehensive planner to use for a real group when you are in practice.

Group Planner

Part one: preliminary planning decisions

Who are the service users?

• Agency?

• Service-user group?

continued

43

- Target group?

- Age?

What are their unmet needs? Why might their unmet needs be met more appropriately in a group than otherwise?

What general needs might they have as regards personal frontiers and preoccupying concerns?

In thinking about the potential target group, have I considered anti-oppressive practice (e.g. is membership of the group denied to anyone without good reason)?

What purpose would the group have:

- for the agency?

- for the service users?

Is there common ground out of which a *contract* could be developed?

Agency issues
Whose permission do I need in order to run this group (practice teacher, on-site supervisor, line manager)?

What resources do I need?

From where or whom shall I obtain my referrals?

What do I need to do to win the support of colleagues?

Who do I need to inform:

- of the group's existence and aims?

- of members' attendance and performance?

Structure of the group
Where will the group meet?

What is the proposed size of the group?

What is to be the duration of the group: How many sessions? Length of each session?

Will there be constancy of membership?

In thinking about the structure of the group, have I considered anti-oppressive practice (e.g. are the venue and timings of the group accessible to everyone)?

Composition
What issues of power do I need to consider as regards group balance (such as ethnicity, gender, class or religious tradition)?

continued

Are there any characteristics that would exclude a potential member (e.g. in an acute state of crisis, or very disorganised or disruptive)?

In what respects am I aiming for a homogeneous group and in what ways would it be desirable to have a heterogeneous group?

What mix of member characteristics am I looking for ideally?

In thinking about the composition of the group, have I considered anti-oppressive practice (e.g. have I thought about the implications of one person being in an obvious minority)?

ACTIVITY **2.7**

Thinking about the service users you identified at the end of Chapter 1 (Activity 1.6), imagine you are planning a group for them. Use the format of the Group Planner to take you through the preliminary planning decisions.

CHAPTER SUMMARY

- In this chapter we have suggested that the starting point in planning any group project is the consideration of the unmet needs of service users where groupwork might be an appropriate method of provision.

- Having decided that there is a group of people for whom a groupwork project would be feasible and useful, it should be easy for you to formulate an aim for your group.

- In planning your group it will be important for you to be aware of how a group might be structured, giving thought to issues of size, frequency, duration and composition, including questions, for example, of age, class, race and gender. Most of these factors exist on a continuum with opposites at either end, and having an understanding of how these different factors influence group performance will help you to come up with a balance of them that best serves the group purpose.

- You will not be able to run a successful group without the support of your colleagues and your agency. It is important to think through the concerns that your managers and colleagues might have, in order to get them to express them openly and to be able to discuss them in a way that is neither precious nor defensive.

FURTHER READING

Benson, J (2001) *Working More Creatively with Groups*, 2nd edition. London: Routledge.

This book has a useful, easy-to-follow chapter on planning decisions, with good use of tables.

Brown, A (1992) *Groupwork*, 3rd edition. Aldershot: Arena.

This has a good, easy-to-follow chapter on planning a group.

Doel, M and Sawdon, C (1999) *The Essential Groupworker*. London: Jessica Kingsley.

This book introduces planning decisions through the use of 12 dimensions, each of which comprises a continuum joining opposites, e.g. open/closed.

Whitaker, DS (1985) *Using Groups to Help People*. London: Routledge.

Whitaker, DS (2001) *Using Groups to Help People*, 2nd edition. Hove: Brunner-Routledge.

We are giving references for both editions of this text as, although they both contain excellent advice on the necessary decisions when planning a group, in the first edition this is done considerably more comprehensively, having three chapters devoted to the subject, including a full chapter on taking the work setting into account.

Chapter 3

Facilitation and co-facilitation

Introduction

In this chapter we will introduce you to facilitating groups, including helping you understand just *what* you may be facilitating, depending on the aim of the group. We will help you to get a sense of *being* a group facilitator by considering your style and how you develop it. At the heart of the chapter is the link between personal awareness and facilitator style. We will look in detail at tasks introduced in Chapter 1 associated with planning, monitoring and maintaining groups, and at the skills associated with intervening in groups, including listening and questioning, and six categories of intervention. We will discuss some of the advantages in working with a co-facilitator and some of the pitfalls. It is worth bearing in mind that the impact and influence of a facilitator begins right at the start of planning a group, in your language, manner and relationships, not just when you walk in to meet the group at the first meeting; your facilitation style and choice of interventions will influence every aspect of your groupwork practice.

Facilitation is a complex art that brings all the facets of being human together to try to model and to learn ways of valuing, communicating with and treating each other more humanely. Planning, developing and working with a group to provide purposeful group experiences is not just one skill, but is an accumulation of skills and experience, combined with a willingness to practise and seek feedback and supervision in order to develop good practice. Paradoxically, the more you experience and learn about facilitation, the more you realise how little you know about the complexity of human interaction. Facilitation is used in many sectors, including business, education, therapy and personal growth, as well as within health and social services. There are many proponents of the art and as many books and websites giving hints, tips and advice (see Further reading). Hogan (2003, p1) suggests:

> There is magic in facilitation, in capturing the ideas of participants and enabling individuals to harness their own energies, skills and group wisdom. At deeper levels, it is about helping people engage in, manage, and cope creatively with the rapid changes within themselves and their communities.

Heron (1999, p13) suggests that facilitator style:

> transcends rules and principles of practice, although it takes them into account and is guided by them. There are good and bad methods of facilitating any given group, but there is no one right and proper method. There are innumerable valid approaches, with a style, language and ethics to match.

Your style will be grounded in your own values and principles, but will be tempered and expanded as you develop your self-awareness, explore the areas of which you were unaware previously and learn from different groups. What, then, does good group facilitation look like? What does it feel like when you are on the receiving end of it? What sort of training, skills or support do you need to develop as a facilitator? Heron (1999, p335) calls facilitator style *a person's signature in action* and suggests that it cannot be acquired but is revealed as behaviour becomes more and more authentic.

RESEARCH SUMMARY

A study by Lieberman et al. (1973, cited in Coyne and Diederich, 2013) established the four basic functions of a group facilitator as caring, affection, acceptance and support. Burlingame and Beecher (2008, cited in Coyne and Diederich, 2013) found that facilitator characteristics of personal warmth, empathy and openness were related to positive therapeutic outcomes. None of this will come as a surprise to those familiar with the work of Rogers (1957).

Personal awareness

Personal awareness is a core requirement for social workers and is also one of the essential elements of good facilitation. It can be useful to think of three zones or areas of awareness and to practise developing competence in accessing and learning from each.

- *Zone one: Attention* out: *focused on behaviour, beliefs and on the outside world.*

- *Zone two: Attention in: focused on thoughts, feelings and sensations.*

- *Zone three: Attention focused on fantasy.*

(Burnard, 1990, p23)

Personal or self-awareness is the gradual and continuous process of noticing and exploring your zones with the intention of developing personal and interpersonal understanding in relation to others.

Developing personal awareness

The Johari window (Figure 3.1) offers a dynamic model with which to explore your personal awareness and to see how others see you. It was developed to help people explore their personal and interpersonal relationships.

Johari illustrates the effects of *self-disclosure* (dotted line) and *feedback* (dashed line) in increasing the *arena* (grey) that represents your personal and interpersonal awareness. The arena quadrant represents things that are known both to you and to others. For example, a person may know your name and so do you. The arena window represents facts about you, and your feelings, desires and emotions. When you first meet a group, this area is small. It can increase in one of two ways: by people finding out more about you – by observing you or by you telling them – so that the dotted line moves downwards, or by you receiving feedback from the group, so that the dashed line moves to the right. We all have different arenas in different parts of our lives; in your family life your arena will be bigger than in your working life. The bigger your arena, the more authentic and real you can be as a facilitator; you are less anxious about revealing your identity within a group because you have already told colleagues about yourself. You will be more relaxed about how you are seen, because you have invited and experienced feedback about yourself. This is important for facilitation with groups. If your arena stays small, you might feel safer yourself, but you are more likely to behave in a discriminatory or oppressive way (whether consciously or unconsciously).

Let us look at why this is. Our hidden window and unseen area usually contain things about ourselves that we are anxious about revealing or have not attempted to face or ask about in ourselves, because we are not sure of receiving a positive reaction. Our own fear may lead us to demonstrate a dislike or to discriminate against someone with a characteristic we find difficult to own or fear in ourselves. It is a form of self-protection or denial of ourselves, usually because we find something too painful or difficult to acknowledge. We can internalise these discriminatory stereotypes and apply them to ourselves as internal oppression. We have a professional responsibility to be constantly vigilant about developing our awareness in order to minimise these possibilities for ourselves and for others. Now explore Johari for yourself.

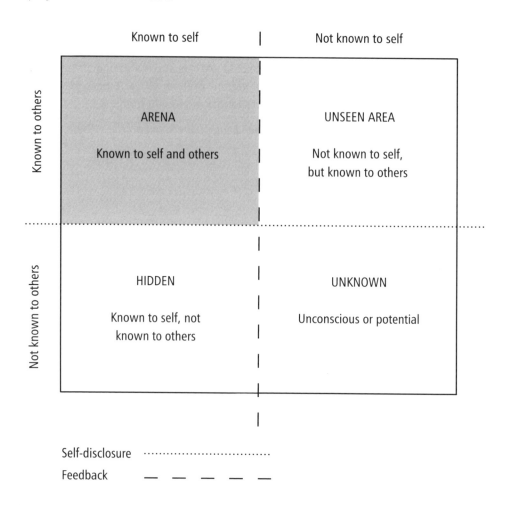

Figure 3.1 The Johari window

ACTIVITY 3.1

For this activity you will need to work with a few other people. Each of you should draw your own Johari window. Fill the 'arena' box with the things that both you and the others know about you and in the 'hidden' box write in some things that you would like the others to know about you and yet they don't. Now share your drawing with the others and invite them to tell you things about you that you do not know. Do the same for them.

Note that you should work carefully and respect the level of risk and disclosure each of you wishes to take. If you find yourself anxious and unwilling to participate in parts of the exercise, then don't; it is important to value your defences. However, ask yourself and note down why, and what you found difficult or scary to hear or reveal, as there are often links between our own defences, our ability to work or facilitate and our potential to discriminate.

Now, discuss how you felt doing each part of the exercise, including noting any surprises or moments of anxiety. Did you manage to open your arena? How did it feel? Did you all find the same bits easy or difficult? Could you repeat the exercise with other colleagues?

> ### COMMENT
>
> *In your conversations you may have found yourself revealing personal information about yourself, including your personal principles and beliefs. Your work with Johari can be considered 'work in progress' – changing as you develop confidence, skill and knowledge of your style.*

Facilitator tasks

To facilitate is to shape and conduct groups by managing the group content and the process, by making interventions to help make sense of, illuminate or steer what is happening in the group. Interventions are all the things you might do or say, or not do or say, during the whole life of a group, from idea through planning to conclusion. They are applicable for all types of groups, meetings or learning activities. In general, you will need to manage all aspects of the group, including opening and closing, timekeeping or working within the agreed contract.

In Chapter 1 we identified four tasks for a group facilitator: planning, intervening, monitoring and maintaining. In this chapter we discuss each in turn, but give priority to intervening and consider in depth the categories of intervention. Your facilitator style, including the manner, pace and language you choose, affects all other tasks and your approach will model your intentions everywhere; we are considering *your* signature in action.

Planning

We discussed preliminary planning decisions in Chapter 2. However, planning is an activity in which you will engage throughout the life of the group. Doel and Sawdon (1999) point to *the need both to plan carefully and yet to be able to set all those plans to one side* (p71). You will need to be prepared to change your plans as you go along, as you take into account and respond to the way in which the group changes and develops – that is, in anticipation and response to processes happening in the group. We look at group processes in Chapter 5 and at planning decisions concerning the group programme in Chapter 6.

Intervening

Creating a supportive environment
You will need to take responsibility for creating a supportive environment and to state and/or negotiate boundaries. There are personal and interpersonal issues in every group, whether articulated or not. They include the elements that make up who we are and how we function, including our gender, age, faith, ethnicity, and sexual and cultural identity, as well as communication styles, personality and learning preferences. Other process issues concern the cultural norms of participants, the group's stage of development, and relationships and agreements, both stated and unstated, inside and outside the group. For best practice the facilitator needs to take responsibility for managing all of these elements. First, here are some skills to help you begin.

Listening and questioning are two intervention skills that you need to develop.

- **Listening** links in with your developing self-awareness. As you become more adept at just listening and noticing in each of your zones of awareness, you will be less inclined to react too quickly or interpret or dismiss things that you hear. Real listening is based on the intention to do one of four things: to understand someone, to learn something, to enjoy someone or to give help or solace. As a facilitator you need to listen with your head for information and your heart for feelings. Be prepared to take a little more time to listen and practise becoming comfortable with pauses and short periods of quiet.

- **Questioning** dances with listening. You are trying to make sense of, and to understand, what is happening in a group, often without making sense or jumping to conclusions too soon. In her basic facilitation toolkit, Hogan (2003) places questioning at the heart of facilitation. Take time to explore different types of questions, for example closed and open questions. Also, choosing the right questions is really important, and you might usefully spend time imagining and framing questions that you might wish to use before a group session. A final note here is to remember that, as questions vary, so too do ways of answering.

> *While helping group members adhere to agreed ground rules, a facilitator needs to be aware of the diverse communication styles between different individuals and cultures. Communication may be direct, fast, hesitant, ponderous and/or repetitive.*
>
> (Hogan, 2003, p70)

Categories of intervention

We have found the six categories identified by Heron (1989) very helpful and have adapted them here. They were originally developed for one-to-one work, but are equally applicable for group facilitation. Think of them as any piece of behaviour, body language or verbal expression that you make, while openly assisting other human beings to learn and to develop as autonomous self-directing and informed people. Your intention is at the heart of all interventions and you need to be as adept at receiving all categories as you are at giving or making them. The categories are: *supportive, catalytic* (encouraging self-directed learning) and *cathartic* (valuing emotion) and *informing, confronting* (pointing out behaviour that is restrictive for the person or the group) and *prescribing*. The majority of participants in Six Category Workshops assess themselves as being weakest in cathartic and confronting interventions. This is likely to be because our society is repressive of the emotions of grief, fear and anger (Heron, 1989). This means we get very little experience of seeing, receiving or making these interventions during our childhood and adolescence. We will therefore look at them in detail and give brief explanations of the others. For further reading and more comprehensive exercises, see Burnard (1990) and Heron (1999).

- **Being supportive** – This is at the heart of all interventions and affirms the worth and value of all the individuals in the group, including their qualities, attitudes or actions. Supportive interventions include giving free attention, listening, soft eye contact and making reflective statements.

- **Being catalytic or encouraging self-directed learning** – Your intention is to encourage self-awareness and self-directed learning and living. You use supportive interventions and allow and assist group members to explore issues without needing to make sense or to come to any conclusions.

- **Valuing emotion or being cathartic** – These interventions seek to enable group members to discharge – to abreact – painful emotion, primarily grief, fear or anger, by being supportive and not pushing, but by giving value to an emotional response. Three important aspects of being human are our capacities to love and be loved, to choose and to be chosen, and to understand and be understood. Heron (1989) argues that, when these capacities are frustrated or frozen in childhood or through life experiences, grief, fear and anger are generated and repressed, causing compulsive and distorted behaviour. Parents and teachers who have themselves been brought up to hide and suppress emotions and feelings can perpetuate this repression. Houston (1990) talks about this by suggesting that we have been brought up to have bad feelings about bad feelings and generally suppress them. One of the aims of good group facilitation is to create the environment in which emotions are valued and space is provided, if appropriate, for the release of feelings, including fear and anger. However, this is not always as easy to facilitate because our own experiences of childhood and upbringing, and our relationship with our emotions, may be a little out of line or distorted too. The fear of someone having strong emotions – for example, being very angry or weeping and sobbing in a group we are facilitating – is a common anxiety for trainee facilitators. This anxiety is directly linked to our relationship with our own 'big feelings' and our ability to express them ourselves. We are not suggesting that every social work group will, or indeed should, be dealing explicitly with emotional release, as in therapy – more that emotions are central to all our learning and experience, and need to be valued and allowed space if appropriate. You never know for sure when you are going to activate an emotional response in yourself or for a group member; because we can't stop feelings, we can only learn that we have choices about how we respond to them. What you can do is to undertake to work with your own emotions and to value the expression of them, so that you see and experience good practice. Sometimes, by revisiting our childhood survival responses, we realise we can respond differently as adults. This, in turn, will build your confidence so that you are not so frightened of others engaging in emotional expression. Personal tutorials or supervision are both appropriate places for identifying and finding help around this issue. You may also find that personal development groups and individual therapy may assist learning in this area.

- **Informing** – Your intention is to be supportive and provide information, knowledge or meaning at the level it is required, by checking out with the group or individual what they need or require.

- **Prescribing or seeking to direct someone's behaviour** – Your intention here is to seek to direct behaviour either of an individual or of members of the group in a supportive manner without stepping on or removing their right to make their own decisions. Your intention would be to draw attention to the consequences of certain behaviour and to suggest an alternative or alternatives.

- **Confronting unhelpful behaviour** – Your intention is to help the individual or group to raise their consciousness of some limiting attitude or behaviour of which they are relatively unaware, and to do this in a supportive way. This is the only category of intervention that you do without permission or in an unsolicited manner, and it is this, as well as our lack of practice, that makes it difficult. Be sure that your intention is to be helpful, not hurtful. Confrontation is only helpful if undertaken with real care for the other person. We do not know for sure how people will take our confrontation because we are offering them some information about them of which they may be unaware. Because we don't know (and fear the worst!) we skew confrontations in two ways. Either we go 'over the top' in our anxiety to justify ourselves and in our readiness to fight back and so demolish a person's character, or we never get to the point at all and dither about around the point we are trying to make. Our anxiety this time causes us to be ready to back down and make little of it. We need to recognise that good confrontation is a very loving and supportive intervention, and we urge you to practise *giving and receiving* confrontations. Practice will help you grow in courage, clarity and expertise and, by receiving supportive confrontations and feeling the benefit, you will fear less. In a group you may choose to confront in front of the whole group (if you are sure that it is beneficial for both the recipient and the group) or you may decide to negotiate a time and place outside the group for giving your feedback. Here is a sequence for a good confrontation.

1. Decide upon the specific behaviour you wish to highlight with a clear reason why you think it is restricting or limiting the person or the group.

2. Check out that the person is ready or prepared to receive your feedback by asking him or her.

3. Be specific about how you want the person to behave differently.

4. Say what you have decided clearly and succinctly no more than two to three times.

5. Describe the behaviour and not the person, i.e. you say, 'you do this', rather than 'you are this sort of a person'.

6. Give time for your confrontation to be received and try not to get into justification or rescue.

7. Then let go and shut up.

It is useful to give time and space for your intervention to be received and digested, because this may be new and surprising information for the recipient, or it is possible that you might be a little wide of the mark or even wrong. You might wish to offer time for talking through your confrontation after it has been digested. Remember, as with all of these interventions, it is in learning to receive an intervention (as you tried in offering feedback in the exercise with Johari) that you learn how to make them.

ACTIVITY 3.2

Using the six-category intervention self- and peer-assessment chart in Table 3.1, assess your ability to deliver and receive each category and record them. Then ask colleagues for their assessment of your abilities. Do this now and perhaps at intervals throughout your training.

COMMENT

Remember that it is in the receiving of interventions that you can learn most how to give an intervention. Sometimes when we are training we are so concerned to learn how to 'do' things we may forget to remember to receive.

Date:	Self-assessment 1 (poor) to 5 (very good)		Peer-assessment 1 (poor) to 5 (very good)	
	Giving	Receiving	Giving	Receiving
Being supportive Giving free attention, good listening, soft eye contact and reflective statements.				
Catalytic (encouraging self-discovery) Supportive + allowing exploration using reflective, open questions without needing to make sense.				
Cathartic (valuing emotion) Supportive + giving value to emotion and then staying with the person and not judging. Working to their time not yours.				
Informing Supportive + checking out level of information needed or given. Their need not yours.				
Prescribing Supportive + clarity of intention seeking to direct behaviour without talking over with 'shoulds' or 'oughts'.				
Confronting Supportive + raising awareness about some limiting attitude or behaviour using direct feedback, but not making a personal attack.				

Table 3.1: Intervention and suggestions for helpful behaviour

Source: Adapted from Heron (2001)

Facilitator styles

Heron (1989) has identified six dimensions of facilitator style. They provide a useful reference with which to consider the range of possible options open to facilitators for shaping and setting the tone of a group experience. Different intervention skills are required to facilitate each dimension with differing group experiences resulting from each; there is no 'right' or 'wrong'. Burnard (1990, p181) has placed the dimensions in a framework.

- **Directive or non-directive** – The facilitator clearly directs the group or encourages the group to direct and make decisions itself.

- **Interpretive or non-interpretive** – The facilitator offers the group interpretations of its behaviour or encourages the group to interpret its own behaviour.

- **Confronting or non-confronting** – The facilitator challenges the group or encourages the group to challenge itself.

- **Cathartic or non-cathartic** – The facilitator encourages the release of emotion in the group or steers it into less emotional territory.

- **Structuring or unstructuring** – The facilitator uses exercises, activities and games to bring structure, or works in a more informal way.

- **Disclosing or non-disclosing** – The facilitator shares her or his own thoughts and feelings or withholds them.

ACTIVITY 3.3

Study the dimensions. Reflect on your experience of being in groups where the different dimensions were in evidence in the style of facilitation. What was your response to the different approaches?

COMMENT

At the beginning of the life of a group you may find structuring, interpretive and directive styles are helpful but, as the group matures and grows in trust and confidence, you can steer the group towards confronting, cathartic and the non-directive and non-interpretive dimensions.

Monitoring

Monitoring is all of the tasks that help you and your colleagues understand how the group is working and developing, so that you are gathering information and making changes as and if needed. Listening, reflecting, talking through and note-taking may all be involved, both alone and with co-facilitators, group members, colleagues and other professionals as appropriate. Supervision is important for monitoring. Try to monitor and give attention to each zone of your awareness from a personal, individual, interpersonal and group level. How am I reacting and what am I feeling? What is going on with each individual? What is going on between individuals? Is there anything happening at the level of the whole group, perhaps an atmosphere of hostility, of sadness, of happiness, of success? Remember that you can involve group participants in this process too – providing opportunities for reflection, and verbal and written feedback, as well as discussion in the group. It is essential to build in and plan time for review meetings in between group meetings.

Maintaining

Maintaining includes all the tasks around the edge of the group meeting time. It can be helpful to look at three general (but overlapping) sets of maintenance tasks: practical, professional and membership.

Practical tasks

These are all the things you need to do to make sure the venue you have chosen and room you will use are appropriate and supportive for the group you are running. If you have decided on a particular venue and addressed any *constraints* (Douglas, 2000, p25) you then need to look at the details. Before the group begins, can you get into the building? Is there anyone else booked into the room before you? If there is a prior booking, is there a long-enough changeover time? It should be your intention to create a comfortable and welcoming space for your group. The lighting, heating and ventilation are important. You will need to consider seating and room layout, including how the chairs are arranged, access and space for people with disabilities, and confidentiality issues if the building is multi-use and there are other people working in the building at the same time as you. Confidentiality and noise may be an issue if the walls are very thin and you do not wish to be overheard or interrupted. In the room itself, think about creating the right atmosphere with information or posters. Consider how someone from a different culture from yours might perceive the building. Is the decor Eurocentric? Would someone from a minority group feel comfortable here or would they feel they did not belong? Bring flipcharts if you intend to record or do activities that require writing or drawing, as well as crayons, pencils and water-solvent pens. How and if you can and wish to display or stick sheets to the walls must be checked out too. You will need to think about arranging refreshments, such as water and hot drinks, including coffee and some herb and fruit teas, as well as fresh milk. Access to a kitchen area can be helpful. The care you take in setting the scene gives a powerful message about how you value the people in the group. Hogan (2003) lists room preparation, readiness of you and the room, the room layout, music and mood (if appropriate), refreshments, food and displays as important practical considerations. Doel (2006) has identified that the success of any one group often depends on very time-consuming practicalities, including:

- securing sufficient funding;
- allocating time to prepare and run a group and, more importantly, getting the timing of a group right for sufficient people to be able to attend;
- choice of venue and access;
- transport for individuals to and from a venue;
- health and safety, including the provision of first aid, the consideration of fire hazards and access for people with disabilities, some of whom may be wheelchair users;
- a list of all the people you might be expecting to attend the group, with contact details, so you know when everyone has arrived.

A group will have a set duration, so having a clock set to the correct time, visible to you and the group, is useful. As the workshop starts and as people arrive, you will need to record who is present. A 'sign-in sheet' can be made available near the refreshments or on a table at the side. At the end of the group the practical tasks will include clearing up and rearranging furniture if needed.

Professional tasks

Included here are all the practical things that you might need to do yourself or with colleagues and other professionals to prepare for facilitating the group, for ongoing monitoring and review, and for ending or completing a group. Preparing yourself alone or with your co-facilitator needs to start well before the day of the group. You will need to read case notes, make decisions about group membership and be clear about your reasons for inclusion and exclusion. You may need to try out exercises or games you intend to use. On the day, try to give yourself at least 15–30 minutes to prepare yourself and your co-facilitators before group members arrive.

Membership tasks

Membership tasks may need your attention before and after the group meets. As we will see in the next chapter, meeting with potential members before a group begins has been found to be helpful. You may need to do some work at the margins of the group, for example with members or their families. Following up reasons for absenteeism may also be required.

ACTIVITY 3.4

Think back to your imaginary group from Chapter 2 (Activity 2.3, pages 32–3) and see if you can think of the maintenance tasks that would help you to organise and run the group. Discuss each category with your colleagues and compare notes.

COMMENT

All three categories of maintenance tasks require time and the last two require you to organise communication with other people; it can be tempting but ill-advised to miss them out. Maintenance tasks that are not attended to thoroughly may 'bite' you later, because they are brought up, or 'emerge', as an issue in a group.

Schimmel and Jacobs (2013) suggest a number of essential skills for good facilitation:

- **Flexibility** – The facilitator needs to be able to 'dance with the group', adjusting the programme in response to what is happening. Sometimes it will become clear that something planned is not working and the facilitator needs to change tack or something will arise in the group dynamic that was not anticipated but provides a good opportunity to move the group on.

- **Engagement skills** – The facilitator needs to be able to keep all the members involved all the time, even when the focus in not directly upon them individually. Discussion focused on one individual can be widened to include others ('This links with what you were saying, yesterday, Josh') and exercises need to be kept interesting, relevant and fairly short. Making sure that as many of the senses as possible are stimulated will help.

- **Good questioning skills** – Many of the skills that you have developed in working with individuals and families will be useful. 'How did you feel then?' is a better question than 'What happened next?'. Try to formulate questions that take the group on, such as 'How might the group help with that?', 'What have you tried in the past that has worked for you?'

- **Use of the eyes** – It is impossible to work with the whole group without looking at all the members, even when the focus is on just one person. Good facilitators are continually scanning the group to see how others are reacting. Have you noticed that a good lecturer is always aware of you and responds to you as an individual, regardless of the size of the class? The good facilitator will also use verbal and non-verbal signals to get group members to pay attention to the other members and not focus only on the facilitator or on whoever is speaking.

- **Use of the voice** – We tend to speak more quietly, stumble and mumble when we are nervous. You need to use your voice to project yourself and to demonstrate confidence, enthusiasm, interest and caring.

- **Motivational skills** – Always project your belief that people can succeed and can change for the better.

- **Cutting off** – You need to be able to interrupt and redirect effectively, if you are to avoid some members dominating, monopolising, shifting the focus unhelpfully or just rambling on. You may find it useful to explain to the group at the outset that you will need to do this from time to time, so that everyone gets a chance to speak, to get back on track or because of what is being said.

- **Drawing out** – Conversely, you will also need to get people to elaborate on what they have said or to help quieter members to contribute without feeling that they are being pounced upon. Often strategies such as getting the conversation to go around (turn taking) or using written exercise or movement can be helpful.

Co-facilitation

Groupwork facilitation offers opportunities for learning through an apprenticeship model. Perhaps one of the most significant advantages of learning to facilitate is that you can watch and participate gradually by co-facilitation or co-working. This is one of the reasons why we recommend this model for beginning groupworkers.

Whether to facilitate a group alone or with others is a decision that you need to make in the early stages of your planning and, if you decide that you should work with others, your co-workers should be involved from the start. There are a number of practical factors that may influence that decision. One factor might be the availability of someone with whom to work. Another might be the size of the planned group: generally speaking, larger groups call for more facilitators. The type of activity planned could be another factor; for example, outdoor pursuits might require a higher facilitator/member ratio for safety reasons. Hodge (1985), in a useful pamphlet, describes the potential gains and possible problems arising from working with a co-worker. Brown (1992) gives similar guidance but divides the benefits between those that arise for the group and those that arise for the workers.

Co-working: potential gains

We combine the guidance from both Hodge (1985) and Brown (1992) regarding the benefits of co-working in Table 3.2.

Benefits for the group	Benefits for the facilitators
Facilitation resources available to the group are enriched – styles, personalities, experiences, knowledge.	More than one view about what is happening in the group is available.
Group members experience the concern or interest of at least two people in authority.	Co-workers can support and counsel each other, and can provide feedback to each other on their performance.
Group members have more than one facilitator to test themselves against or with whom they can identify.	The impact of the dependent behaviour of group members can be shared.
The facilitators can model specific social and interactional interpersonal skills and the working relationships.	If one groupworker loses touch or control, or becomes overly tired, the other can take over.
Co-facilitators can provide an improved balance for the group in terms of ethnicity, gender and other characteristics and can model positive working relationships between these groups.	Facilitation tasks can be shared, e.g. one monitors/one records, one leads 'up front'/ one looks after emotional needs, etc.
If one groupworker is ill or unavailable, the group meeting can still take place.	Co-working provides training opportunities for less experienced groupworkers.

Table 3.2: Co-working: potential gains

Source: Adapted from Hodge (1985) and Brown (1992)

Co-working: potential pitfalls

However, co-working adds a further level of complexity to the task of facilitation. Now the facilitator has to be aware and take account of the co-facilitator in addition to the group and the individual members. Hodge (1985) points to the pitfalls.

- Inadequate preparation by the co-facilitators leads to mismatching perceptions of task and role.

- The co-workers have irreconcilable differences in theoretical orientation.

- They have differences of opinion about the techniques, skills or styles required.

- They are in competition.

- There are agency-related tensions where facilitators are from different agencies.

- They fail to build in planning and review sessions, and this leads to discrepancies in perceptions of task, role and group development.

- The co-workers are split off by group members.

These potential difficulties led Benson (2001) to counsel beginning groupworkers against co-working. However, we disagree. We consider that, provided time is taken to develop trust and confidence with a potential co-worker or colleague, the benefits listed above far outweigh the disadvantages. In our experience, beginning groupworkers feel much more confident in a co-working role and we recommend building some strategies into groupwork projects that will help to overcome the potential difficulties. Having an additional person involved in the project, who acts in a supervisory or mentoring role, can be very helpful in sorting out the problems that can arise between co-workers, in addition to providing an objective 'distanced' view of what is happening in the group itself. We will return to this topic in greater detail in Chapter 8. Good preparation for the task of co-working is also very important, and clear and honest communication between the co-facilitators will go a long way towards preventing problems before they occur. Hodge (1985) provides a long list of questions that intending co-workers can work through in preparation for facilitating a group together. We reproduce just a few of these in the following exercise.

ACTIVITY 3.5

Find someone with whom you could imagine yourself co-facilitating a group and work together through the following activity.

In this exercise work as if you are prospective co-workers.

The purpose is to think through the issues and circumstances that have to do with working together on a groupwork programme.

Work through one question at a time. Take turns in responding to each question.

Do not feel hurried; take time to discuss each other's responses.

Do not move on to the next question until each of you feels that sufficient has been said; at the same time, try not to overload each other with more information than can comfortably be absorbed.

Differences and how they are to be used/managed

(a) In the relationship between us, consider the following.
- *What are each of our strengths/assets as facilitators?*

- *Where are our possible deficits as facilitators?*

- *In working together, what issues do we need to take account of as regards gender, ethnicity, religious tradition, class, age, (dis)ability, sexuality, etc? Are there likely problems that we can predict? What strategies do we need to adopt?*

- *Are there any other issues of power differential between us, for example status, grade, length of experience?*

- *Can either of us envisage a situation in which we could not support the other, or in which either of us might feel let down by the other?*

ACTIVITY **3.5** *continued*

(b) In the groupwork process, consider the following.
* *What for each of us is the most congenial way of handling disagreements with other people? How do we usually behave when we come into conflict with others?*

* *How negotiable do we believe the programme is with the group members?*

* *What is our attitude to rules and sanctions?*

* *What is the preferred facilitation style for each of us?*

* *Are we going to divide up the facilitation work? If so, how? Who will deal with discipline, keeping to task, support, emotional issues, etc?*

* *What for each of us is the worst thing that could happen . . . and the best?*

COMMENT

Preparing to work with a co-facilitator is every bit as important as the other preparation work that you do. You need to take time to build trust between you, to reach out for feedback and to explore issues and hidden areas. The Johari window (see Figure 3.1) is a useful tool to use.

Now we can add the second part of the Group Planner we introduced in Chapter 2.

Group Planner

Part two: facilitation issues

What are the principal tasks that will fall to me as groupworker?

Shall I work alone or with a co-worker?

If working with a co-worker, what issues do we need to explore before working together?

These include:

* differences in power (consider gender, religious tradition, culture, grade, class, ethnicity, sexual orientation, physical difference, age, etc.);

* differences in theoretical orientation;

* differences of opinion about techniques skills or styles required;

* competitiveness;

* agency-related tensions if we are from different agencies;

continued

- personal issues, particularly those related to the group context;

- division of roles and tasks;

- when and where debriefing sessions are to take place, if there is to be a co-worker;

- if there is to be anyone else involved (e.g. outside speakers) and the preparation needed regarding their involvement.

ACTIVITY 3.6

As before, return to your imaginary group and complete this section of the Group Planner.

CHAPTER SUMMARY

- In this chapter we have suggested that your facilitation style or 'personal signature' is grounded in your own values and principles and, more importantly, that your style is tempered and expanded as you develop self-awareness. We have offered models, theories and activities to assist your personal development.

- You will know how important it is to pay attention to personal, professional and participant requirements and practical details before, during and after a group. We have looked in detail at the tasks of planning, monitoring and maintaining groups, and linked these with three zones of awareness.

- Developing your style relies on your willingness to try out and develop both giving and receiving interventions. Intervention skills are considered in some detail, including listening, questioning and Heron's (1989) six categories of intervention: supportive, catalytic, cathartic, confronting, informative and prescriptive. You have a self- and peer-assessment sheet to enable you to practise now and as your style develops.

- The key to understanding facilitation is to remember that your facilitation style is you in action and how you behave will influence every aspect of your groupwork practice.

- You may find it useful to work with a co-facilitator. There are many benefits in co-working a group and also some potential pitfalls. However, the latter can be avoided through good planning and open, honest communication.

Doel, M and Sawdon, C (1999) *The Essential Groupworker.* London: Jessica Kingsley.

This has a good chapter on co-working.

Heron, J (2001) *Helping the Client: A creative practical guide.* London: Sage.

This is an updated edition of *Six Category Intervention Analysis* with all the categories explained in detail.

Hogan, C (2003) *Practical Facilitation: A toolkit of techniques.* London: Kogan Page.

This book provides a comprehensive and accessible toolkit for developing facilitation with helpful examples and context. The chapter on 'Cross-cultural and diversity issues' is helpful.

Houston, G (1990) *The Red Book of Groups and How to Lead Them Better*, 3rd edition. London: Rochester Foundation.

This is a book we find useful. There is an excellent reflective chapter called 'Horses for courses' to help you notice how you lead. It has cartoons and is small enough to put in your pocket!

Whitaker, DS (2001) *Using Groups to Help People*, 2nd edition. Hove: Brunner-Routledge.

This has very useful chapters: one on listening, observing and contributing meanings to what happens in groups, another on intervening, and a third on the therapist in the group.

The following contain useful chapters or sections on both co-working and mentoring.

Brown, A (1992) *Groupwork*, 3rd edition. Aldershot: Arena.

Preston-Shoot, M (2007) *Effective Groupwork*, 2nd edition. Basingstoke: Palgrave Macmillan.

Chapter 4
Setting up the group

Introduction

In this chapter, we look at membership negotiation and contracts. Although by now you have made a number of important decisions about the group, its purpose, how it is to be structured and how to secure the support of your managers and colleagues, there is still much to do before the group first meets. You will need to decide how you will go about offering the group to prospective members, how you will ensure that you end up with a group of a workable size, and what understanding you will have with each member about the nature of the group itself.

Offering the group

Sometimes this task is relatively straightforward, especially if you have decided to facilitate a group for service users with whom you are working already. It becomes a little more complicated where it is your colleagues who have the ongoing relationship and you have to rely on them to make the offer, or where your potential members are in the community and you have to advertise, as they may have no existing contact with your agency. In all situations, you must provide clear preliminary information about the purpose and conduct of the group and what the criteria for membership are to be, if any. This is a rather tricky problem. You will remember that, in Chapter 2, we discussed some criteria to be considered in the composition of the group; now we consider how we might select potential members to whom we are to make an offer of a group, either directly or indirectly. It is entirely possible, of course, that the membership will be self-selecting, either because you are going to be working with an existing group, or because you are responding to a request from particular service users for a service. In most cases, however, you will need to have some criteria, to ensure that you target the service appropriately, and to avoid the group being seriously over- or undersubscribed. You can control the number of potential group members by how strictly you define the criteria.

CASE STUDY

Siobhan and Robert's team has decided to provide a support group for people suffering from back pain, of whom there are a very large number in the local area. The team patch is in an area of high deprivation and most of the members will have to travel to the centre by public transport as few have private cars. It is not possible for the team to provide transport. In view of this difficulty, they decide to restrict membership to people living in a relatively small geographical area, close to the centre, where public transport is good. In this way, they calculate, they will be able to control the numbers and ensure that they make provision for the people who will be least inconvenienced by travel. When the group meets, they are surprised and dismayed to find that all the members are white, in spite of the fact that the team area is ethnically diverse. They realise that their decision has had the effect of denying membership to people from minority ethnic groups, most of whom live outside the defined area.

It is OK to have strict criteria, so long as you can justify them in terms of real benefit for service users and you check you are not inadvertently denying access to some people. Decisions that we may make to exclude people based on descriptive attributes (see Chapter 2) are likely to be discriminatory and should be avoided. It is better to say for whom the group is being provided, rather than for whom it is not; it is better if people make their own decisions, based on information that you provide. Usually this will mean a preliminary meeting.

Preliminary meetings

It is good practice to meet with each person before a group begins and a number of authors discuss the advantages of preliminary meetings (Benson, 2001; Brown, 1992; Doel and Sawdon, 1999; Manor, 1986, 1988). You may think that a preliminary meeting with each prospective group member is not necessary, for example where the group already exists or where the members are subject to court orders and have no real choice about attendance. However, Croxton (1974, cited in Manor, 1986, pp22–4) describes a number of *contractual sequences* in which a service user and worker agree to work together. The first stage, *prior conditions*, concerns the issues we have covered in Chapter 2. The second, the *exploratory* stage, begins with the information we receive about the potential members and leads us into making initial contact with those whom we decide to approach with an offer. The third, the *negotiation* stage, starts when we first meet the service user face to face and begin to share expectations, reservations and misconceptions on both sides. Potential group members will have all sorts of expectations about what the group may offer, about you and about the other possible members. We are sure you will remember from learning about individual work that we must start 'where the client is', and you will be aware also of the importance of working in partnership with service users. The fourth stage is the *preliminary contract*. The final three stages, the *working agreement*, *secondary contract* and *termination*, take place with the whole group when it is up and running. For now, we will look at the *negotiation* and *preliminary contracting* stages, pointing to some of the issues you will need to consider.

Negotiating

ACTIVITY **4.1**

You work in a family support setting. You are about to set up a group for the parents of young people who have been involved in repeated petty offending. You have requested referrals from your colleagues. You have asked them to discuss the idea of a group with parents who are having this problem at present and to let you have the names of those who show interest. Your colleagues have identified 12 parents. You are now going to visit them in their homes. List the areas that you think will be important to discuss with them.

COMMENT

Thinking about any negotiation in which we involve ourselves, it is important that we have a clear understanding of what we are committing to. When we buy a car, we want to have information about the model generally and also about the vehicle in question. We may also want to make some assessment of the vendor – in terms of how honest they seem, how trustworthy, etc. The potential group member also needs to be in a position to make an informed judgement about the group on offer.

- **Introductions** – Whatever the venue, it can beneficial for the prospective members to meet you – to put a face to the name. Meetings will be dictated by the individual circumstances of the situation, purpose, clientele, agency, etc. and will also determine whether it is best to meet at the agency, the venue, the service users' homes or elsewhere. Prospective members will want to make some assessment of you, for example how open you are, how warm or how trustworthy. You will need to provide some information about yourself, what your position is in the organisation and what your role is to be in the group. Manor (1986) uses a metaphor of people in a double-decker bus (representing the groupworkers) trying to communicate with people in a van (the prospective members). Not only are the mechanics of communication rather difficult, but also the occupants are coming from two different social systems. An introductory meeting can help both. It will also be of help to you to get an impression of the group members, how they might interact with each other and any special individual characteristics that you may have to take into account.

- **Provision of information about the group** – Clarity is important. The information you give reveals how well you understand the purpose of, and plan for, the group. Detailed information is needed here. People will want to know what benefits the group will have for them individually, what the activities will be and what demands membership will make of them. They will want to know who else is going to be in the group and will already have some strong ideas about people they already know, which may well affect their decision about whether to come. They will want to know whether attending or not attending will affect what happens to their children. Confidentiality will certainly be an issue. Maybe there will be practical issues. How will they get there? Will you pay their travel expenses?

In doing the activity, you probably thought of other issues that we have not yet mentioned. The preliminary meeting can have a number of functions in addition to introductions and providing information.

- **Promoting motivation** – It is important not to set out to *sell* the group. However, if the group members are not well motivated towards the group, especially at this stage, the group will fail. In this initial contact with you, the service users' attitudes will be greatly influenced by their perception of you. If you appear confident, knowledgeable and enthusiastic about the group, this will in itself be a motivator. Demonstrating good listening skills and a supportive intention is helpful too. People frequently have reservations about attendance, no matter how positively they may otherwise feel (we will elaborate on these in the next chapter). It is important to listen carefully to these concerns because they will help shape and improve your planning.

- **Ensuring an actual match between the needs of the members and the services the group will provide** – A meeting is an opportunity to explore the potential members' motivations and to make sure that the group is relevant to their needs. People may have responded to the initial offer of a group for a number of reasons. Not all of these will be appropriate. The individual may be under pressure from someone else – for example, a family member or a referring social worker – and not be assertive enough to refuse. He or she may have unrealistic expectations of the group. Benson (2001) makes the point that it may be helpful to identify specific problems or needs with which the group can help *rather than permit global aspirations or expectations* (p45). It may turn out that the group is not suitable for the prospective member.

- **Individualisation** – Having individual contact with prospective group members will be affirming and validating both for them and for you. Service users will be assured that the purpose of the group is to meet their needs, that they are valued as individuals and that you can hear their concerns. It is much easier for prospective members to express any reservations they may have at this early stage, rather than in the first sessions of the group itself. In fact, if you do not provide them with the opportunity to raise these issues in the comparative safety of a one-to-one meeting, you may not have any other opportunity to deal with them, as they may never attend.

- **Giving people choice** – It is important that people know that they have choices and that their right to choose is a central issue for the group facilitators. Allowing and negotiating around choice is one of the important aspects of being human that we mentioned in Chapter 3, and is central to our philosophy of groupwork as an empowering and democratic method. Your supportive behaviour now will also demonstrate an equivalent willingness to be flexible about decisions to be made during the life of the group. For some individuals the choice can be very limited, for example when the group is an alternative to custody. However, as Doel and Sawdon (1999) argue, a discussion with the prospective member about choice or lack of choice in a preliminary interview can help in resolving some of the issues and address emotions raised, thereby perhaps avoiding this becoming a preoccupation in the group itself.

Contracting

Contracting is widely used in social work with both individuals (for example, Corden and Preston-Shoot, 1987; Egan, 1998; Trevithick, 2005b) and groups. Preston-Shoot (1989, p9) suggests that groupwork contracts generally fall into one of four categories:

> – *preliminary contract: comprising an agreement to survey what is being offered without commitment and to clarify expectations;*
>
> – *primary contract: a mutual agreement based on a common definition of goals;*
>
> – *interim agreement: a trial period either because the aims are not agreed or to establish whether services offered are appropriate to the needs defined;*
>
> – *reciprocal agreements in which workers and members accept that their purposes are not identical but agree to co-operate in helping each other to achieve their different goals.*

Contracts or agreements can be formal or informal, written or verbal. Brown (1992) suggests that the member/worker power relationship varies from group to group and has an impact on the level of negotiability of the group contract. In some groups, the level of member power is high and the level of negotiability is, therefore, also high. In a community group, for example, the members may determine most of the decisions about how the group will run, with the worker facilitating the group through the provision of resources. If, however, member power is low, for example where their attendance is required under a court order, their scope or ability to negotiate is correspondingly low. Nevertheless, even in low member-power groups, cooperative group membership and some level of negotiability need to exist. The worker must be clear and honest about the level of negotiability. Good practice dictates that the facilitators and members should have a clear understanding of the purpose of the group and what everyone can expect of each other. It is better that each individual has an understanding of this before agreeing to join the group, rather than finding later that the group is not tenable for him or her and having to leave prematurely. Some writers, for example Benson (2001), argue for an individual contract for each member; some (e.g. Preston-Shoot, 2007) suggest worker/whole group contracts; although others (e.g. Brown, 1992) suggest both a preliminary contract with each member and then a working agreement when the group is established. Allowing negotiation of individual contracts at the beginning of a group fits with our model of learning and clarifying as an iterative or staged process. It is good practice to provide opportunities at the start of a group for members to reflect on and then reinforce or amend a contract in the face of worker/member or member/member interaction. Before we go on to look at the areas that an agreement might include, you may find the following activity useful.

ACTIVITY 4.2

Identify the strengths and weaknesses in the following example of a written contract for a group of young people leaving care. The group aim is to equip them with the knowledge and skills to live independently.

Group contract

- *Group members will attend all the sessions. Any group member who misses two or more sessions will be deemed to have left the group and will not be able to return.*

- *Group members will turn up on time.*

- *Everyone in the group will keep the content of the sessions confidential.*

- *Group members will treat each other with respect. Members will be non-discriminatory in their verbal and non-verbal interactions.*

- *When one person is speaking, no one else will interrupt.*

- *Group members will trust each other.*

- *There will be no chewing or spitting.*

- *No one will be allowed to stay in the group if under the influence of drink or drugs.*

Imagine you are a member of this group. What aspects of the contract would you welcome and which ones would you resent?

COMMENT

This contract is problematic in a number of ways.

- *It seems very one-sided. A contract has two sides. It involves obligations on the part of the workers as well as the members of the group.*

continued

COMMENT *continued*

- *This contract appears to have been imposed on the members by the workers. Contracts cannot be imposed by one side on the other. They are agreements freely entered into; contracts come about as a result of negotiation between people. Positive use of contracts encourages participation and commitment in the group members. However, this is only likely to be the case where the members of the group feel they own the contract and they will do so only if they have been involved in drafting it.*

- *This seems more like a list of rules imposed by the workers than a contract. As just stated, contracts cannot be imposed on one side by the other. Contracts are negotiated and are not merely lists of rules that the group members have to abide by. The imposition of rules, especially unnecessary rules, sets up immediate potential for conflict in the group. Furthermore, rules can often suppress behaviour that might otherwise emerge and that might provide useful material on which work in the group can take place. Oddly, where members are involved in drawing up the rules for a group, they will often be more rigorous in their expectations of each other than the facilitator might expect.*

- *The conditions set out in a contract should be achievable. You cannot require people to trust each other. You may hope that the content of the sessions will be kept confidential, but it may be too much to expect of a group of young people and to have a confidentiality clause in a contract may set up false expectations.*

- *The contract should be expressed in language that everyone understands. This example contains social work jargon, such as 'non-discriminatory', 'verbal' and 'non-verbal'.*

CASE STUDY

A group was set up with a rule that the young participants were not allowed to wear baseball caps. The reason given by the facilitators was that baseball caps prevented them having eye contact with the young people. Inexperienced groupworkers sometimes make the mistake of responding to what they perceive as a problem by introducing a rule, rather than dealing with the underlying issue. In this case, it might have been much more useful if the topic of baseball caps, or the avoidance of eye contact between the members and facilitators, was an area for discussion in the group.

We now suggest some of the areas to include in your agreement with individual members.

- **The aims for the group as a whole**.

- **The aims and goals for individuals within the group** – These may be different, but should be consistent with the group goals.

- **Guarantees** – What undertakings are being given by the facilitators, regarding their attendance, their commitment, the protection of vulnerable members, resources, etc?

- **What will happen in the group** – What methods/activities will be used? What experiences will the individual have and what will be required of him or her in respect of these, for example in relation to physical activities?

- **Venue, times, duration** – Where and when will the group meet and for how long?

- **Group ground rules** – What rules, if any, are there to be? How negotiable are these to be? Are there any exceptions? What sanctions will there be for rule breaking? (We will discuss ground rules in more detail in Chapter 5.)

- **Confidentiality** – What can the members expect of the workers and of each other?

- **Other contacts** – What is to happen about the service users' contact with other workers in the agency, or indeed with the facilitator(s) outside the context of the group?

Before we leave this discussion on groupwork contracts, Table 4.1 shows an interesting example of how mutual expectations might be contained in a contract, suggested by Benson (2001). Note how Benson uses the softer concept of *expectations* rather than anything harder, such as *conditions*, in this contract example.

OUR EXPECTATIONS OF EACH OTHER	
What you can expect of me	**What I expect of you**
To make available my skills, knowledge and concern to help you make the best of this situation.	To help me create a situation where you can develop, learn, and grow. This means you choose to use me and others appropriately.
To be as honest in everything with you as I can. I will take risks with you and others in saying what I really think and feel.	To be as honest in your dealings with me as you can; to take appropriate risks with your thoughts and feelings.
To be accepting and supportive of you and ready to clear the air through discussion with you.	To take responsibility for yourself, your being here, your growth and learning.
To allow and assist you to develop your own potential, and to satisfy your needs for growth and esteem.	To be accepting and supportive towards me and the others and ready to clear the air when necessary. Our growth is your growth.

Table 4.1: Contract example: Our expectations of each other

Source: Benson (2001, p47)

ACTIVITY **4.3**

Returning again to your imaginary group, write out a draft group contract, i.e. one that you will negotiate with the members as a whole.

COMMENT

There are two ways you can draft a written contract for use with the whole group: you can write a preliminary draft by yourself, on the basis of what you think will be important to group members, and then negotiate it with them, or you can formulate the details of the contract in an early session of the group itself. In the latter case you will still need to have a clear idea of what your requirements are, but you will also need to be prepared to negotiate.

CHAPTER SUMMARY

- In this chapter, we dealt with the activities involved in setting up the group.

- The first of these activities is making the offer of a group project to the potential members, which we can either do directly with people with whom we already have contact, or otherwise have to do by relying on colleagues or advertising.

- Although not all projects start with a preliminary contact between the worker(s) and prospective members, it is now considered to be good practice; we looked at some of the reasons for this and considered what might comprise the topics for such a meeting.

- Again, it is a matter of good practice to have some form of contract or working agreement with the service users. This may be formal or informal, written or verbal, and can be with the members individually, collectively or both. The contract needs to be comprehensive and we looked at some of the issues to be covered; however, it is never set in stone – it may be changed as circumstances demand as the group goes on.

FURTHER READING

Brown, A (1992) *Groupwork*, 3rd edition. Aldershot: Ashgate Publishing.

This book contains useful material on the methods of selection and contracting, including the negotiating stages.

Doel, M and Sawdon, C (1999) *The Essential Groupworker.* London: Jessica Kingsley.

In this you will find an excellent chapter on offering the group and discussion of group agreements.

Douglas, T (2000) *Basic Groupwork*, 2nd edition. London: Routledge.

This text contains some discussion of both selection and use of contracts.

Preston-Shoot, M (1989) Using contracts in groupwork. *Groupwork*, 2: 36–47.

This article, although written some time ago, provides a comprehensive discussion of the use of contracts in groupwork and offers suggestions about their content.

Chapter 5
Group processes

Introduction

This chapter will concentrate on helping you understand group processes in more depth. It will build on the overview, planning and facilitation chapters but will look more closely at the issues and complexity of what *happens* when groups of people get together and what you can do to facilitate a certain outcome or provide a supportive environment for your particular client group. The processes we are concerned with are responses, behaviours and reactions that occur at different 'stages' of a group's life, especially in terms of how these influence our choices about facilitation and the structure from planning to evaluation. These responses can be by one individual through to a 'whole group' reaction. Some 'reactions and responses' will be as a result of all sorts of things that you do or decide not to do in relation to planning, design and content before, in and after groups. Some will be unpredictable; others can be anticipated in the life cycle of a group. It is this very complexity that makes groupwork potentially creative and powerful, and it is for this reason that you need to begin to understand group processes so that you are aware of what may be happening or going to happen in your groups. We have recognised in the first chapter how groups can help with learning. It follows that a good understanding of group processes will also help you when you are learning in groups and indeed when you are being assessed as a member of a group.

We have already discussed some of the advantages of using groupwork to create conditions in which people are able to make changes that will improve their lives in some way. These advantages come about as a consequence of people interacting together and the group providing space for things that one-to-one interventions cannot. Paradoxically, it is exactly these 'magnified dynamics' that may frighten practitioners and prevent groupwork being widely used. Doel (2006, p114) makes the following suggestion:

> *Difficulties in groups and teams are amplified by the complex dynamics involved and their semi-public nature. This is perhaps why the idea of groups and groupwork can seem intimidating.*

Understanding process

Recognising process

Many social work students have difficulty in understanding the concept of 'process' and how it differs from 'content'. It is also quite difficult to explain what we mean by process but, as a phenomenon in groupwork, an understanding and awareness of process is critical. It may be useful to use the example of baking a loaf. If we want to bake bread we need ingredients – flour, yeast, water, salt, at least, and perhaps some fat, milk or flavouring. These ingredients are the content but they do not come together to form bread until they have gone through the processes of mixing, kneading, proving and baking. So these processes that take place change the ingredients so that at the end we have something different – bread. Likewise with groupwork, you should expect process to work in a way that changes the group in some way. Process can work either in favour of the desired outcome for the group or against it. However, just as the baker can alter the processes involved, for example the length of proving, the baking temperature and so forth, the group facilitator can work with the group processes to ensure that a favourable outcome is more likely, as we shall see shortly.

In groupwork, Douglas (2000, p36) explains that all 'process' means:

> *is that there are discernible patterns of behaviour which tend to emerge in groups over time and appear to focus around certain aspects of the group's behaviour.*

The most fundamental process of all, he asserts, is interaction. Douglas (1995) says that the term 'process' is used to mean *all the things, which happen in communication between individuals . . .* **but not the actual words** (p47) (our emphasis). Process concerns what occurs as a *result* of the words.

Benson (2001) explains that *process* is about the *how* of individual and group experience – how people react to certain circumstances or are behaving towards each other, or how the group acts together. It is reflected in the quality of the group experience. We need to understand that there is a difference between content and process. *Content* refers to the *what* of group experience – what people are doing and saying, or what they are going to do next. Content is the substance of what is happening in the group; it is on the surface and can be seen or heard. Process, however, happens below the surface. It can rarely be seen or heard but can, nevertheless, be experienced and felt.

CASE STUDY

After a group has been running for some time, one of the members, Janice, says that she has been disappointed that the group has kept to very safe topics; she had hoped that, by now, people would have started to talk about personal issues. The members of the group react to this statement in different ways. Some of the members ignore it and carry on with their discussion as before. One member of the group, Beth, feels that Janice is right; she remembers shying away when topics became too difficult and now she feels guilty. Other members feel angry and resentful; they have found the group discussion very helpful and think that Janice is being self-indulgent; that she is trying to steer the group towards meeting her particular needs. These feelings result in people acting differently. Some start to ignore Janice. Beth, however, suddenly discloses a piece of very personal information. This leads to her being attacked by another member.

COMMENT

Here we discern both content and process. What Janice says is part of the content of the group. The consequences of what she has said and, in particular, the patterns that arise (for example, Beth always supports her) form part of the process.

ACTIVITY 5.1

This activity will help you identify 'process' and clarify the differences between content and the process issues in situations from your own experience. Select two or three different group situations that you identified in the previous chapters and see if you can differentiate between the content and processes within each.

- **The content** – *When did people arrive? Who was there? What did they do? What did they say? Was there an agenda? Was it followed? What decisions were made? When did they leave?*

- **The process issues** – *What happened next? Consideration of how, when, why. How did the group work together? What emotions arose? Where did they come from? How did people react to what was said? Did they react differently to each other? Were there links between what was said, the emotions and what was said or done next?*

ACTIVITY 5.1 *continued*

Fill in the chart below with some of your own examples.

Content: What did people say or do?	Process: What happened next? How, when and why?	Comment: What did you notice/feel/think?
e.g. Facilitator introduced everyone.	No one got to introduce themselves; some people seemed unhappy with how they were introduced.	Maybe people felt undervalued and a little resentful of the facilitator They seemed ready to jump in to correct any future mistakes.

COMMENT

When you think about it, you are dealing with both content and process all the time – when you realise that what someone has said has more meaning than you first thought; for example, when a service user asks you if you have any children, you realise that he or she may be asking if you have enough experience to be working with that person and so you may try to reassure him or her in some way.

Content questions and the resulting structure you decide upon are the keys to process facilitation. It is this relationship and the links with the resulting process and the management of personal, interpersonal and group process that are the keys to helping people. You aim to provide a supportive environment for people to test, use and explore, and hopefully to understand and change their behaviour and experience.

Process in groups

The concept of process is important in any social work interaction, but is perhaps particularly important when we are working with more than one person at a time, in work with families (see, for example, Crago, 2006) and with groups. All groups have process. When people come together they become aware of each other, and gradually and subtly change in response to each other's behaviour. This happens as well as the reactions and responses to content and structure. We call this phenomenon *group process*. Group process develops primarily as a consequence of the larger number of interactions and interrelationships in the room. Therefore, for example, when we say something in a one-to-one situation, there is only the other person who can respond to it, but when we say or do something in a group, we can set off a chain reaction as people respond to what has happened and then people respond to the various responses. This can make a situation very confusing. What helps us, however, is that, with practice, we are able to spot themes and patterns in the ways that people respond. It is then possible to discern these themes and patterns in the flow of group process. Also, process can be experienced both emotionally and physically, and when you recognise it you are on the first step to developing skills of working with it by becoming more open and receptive to what is happening. Having achieved this awareness you will be in a position to intervene in a way that will influence the process of the group and promote positive change. You can affect the processes by the way you choose to structure and facilitate the content, your interventions being your tools.

Douglas (1995) identifies nine processes that occur in groups: interaction, communication, consequences (what is going on – what follows what), aim setting, the establishment of roles, developing cohesion, discovering and developing resources (e.g. knowledge and skills of individual members), making decisions, and bringing about change (in self, the group or externally).

Douglas (2000, p37) further classifies the processes in groups as follows.

The structural processes:	*Group development*
	Role and status
	Subgroup formation
The operational processes:	*Goal formation*
	Decision-making
	Using resources
The regulating processes:	*Setting norms, standards and values*
	Developing cohesion
	Acquiring influence
	Developing an ethos

Of these, group development may be the most important to understand. As Brown (1992, p100) argues:

> *One of the most profound characteristics of group process is the way in which the whole mood and functioning of a group, the roles, behaviour, communication patterns and interaction of the members can and do change quite dramatically over a period of time.*

Models of group process

There are a number of models that can help us understand group process. We have space for only two. Benson (2001) uses the polarities of *love* and *will*. He uses *love* to refer to the natural human desire to be attached, to be a part of a larger unit and to take part in a social experience larger than oneself. *Will* is the urge to be individual and separate, and to retain one's own identity. All the time in a group, every individual experiences these two competing urges. The love urge manifests itself in things such as making friends, joining in, chatting, sharing and trusting. It also brings with it distortions such as shyness, embarrassment, superficiality, fear of rejection, jealousy and suspicion. The will urge results in behaviour such as people starting things, organising, leading, solving problems and confronting undesirable behaviour. Its counter-side brings about things such as rivalry, stubbornness, selfishness, powerlessness, bullying and apathy. Each individual in the group has to resolve these competing urges in themselves and it is through this resolution that the group finds new behaviours, moves forward, and so grows and matures. Perhaps an illustration from the world of physics will help here. As is shown in Figure 5.1, if two or more forces are acting on an object, the object (in this case the group) will move (provided the forces are not exactly equal and acting in a line in exactly opposite directions).

Whitaker (2001) uses a similar idea of competing forces to explain group process. Whitaker's group focal conflict theory, in simplified terms, works like this. Sometimes an impulse emerges in a group. Whitaker calls this a *disturbing motive*. This can be a wish, a desire or a hope. If there is nothing to stand in its way, this shared wish is openly expressed and becomes a theme for discussion. The group, for example, may wish that the discussion becomes more personal and that the members become more self-disclosing. However, a wish is often accompanied by a fear or guilt and this fights against its emergence. In our example (see the last Case study on page 76), people are frightened that they may be hurt by how others react to their self-disclosure. This is called a *reactive motive*. A conflict therefore arises for which the group must find a solution. The group may find a *restrictive solution*, which deals with the fear at the expense of the wish, or an *enabling solution*, which deals with the fear but also allows the expression of the wish. In this way fears are contained and the group is able to explore the associated impulses and emotions. In our example, a restrictive solution would be for the group to decide that disclosure is far too risky and a norm therefore arises that members do not disclose personal information, keeping only to safe topics. An enabling solution might be the recognition that we all have issues that are difficult to disclose, but that we can help deal with them by bringing them into the open – that it is helpful both for the individual and for others for there to be discussion about the issue. A norm arises in the group that people are respected, valued and treated with care when they make a disclosure. In this way, the group moves to a new level of interaction.

Whitaker argues that conflict can become established in a group where some of the members press for a particular solution (enabling or restrictive) and others in the group fight against it. She terms this *solution conflict.* Whitaker uses group focal conflict theory to

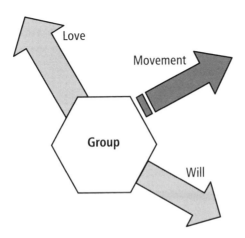

Figure 5.1: Group movement in response to competing forces

explain a number of familiar phenomena in groups: the moods or atmospheres that develop, such as frivolity or depression, and behaviour, which the facilitator may perceive as unhelpful in terms of the group's development, but which is in fact functional, in some way, for the group.

Stages of group development

Groups do change over time and every group has a discernible beginning, middle and an ending phase. The changes that take place over these phases have an effect on the different roles of members, their interaction with each other and their ways of communicating.

RESEARCH SUMMARY

McKenzie (1994, cited in Whitaker 2001) conducted a study of theories of group development and identified 117 authors over a period of almost one hundred years. As Whitaker (2001) suggests, this represents a very large amount of work on just this one aspect of small groups.

Theories of group development generally fall into one of two broad categories: linear models that suppose that groups develop progressively as if in a straight line; and cyclical models that imply that groups' development follows a cycle, going around and around through the various stages but usually reaching a higher level of development each time. This is perhaps better perceived as a spiral rather than a circle. Tuckman's (1965) model is perhaps the best-known linear model. He identified a number of distinct stages of development that he designated as *forming*, *storming*, *norming* and *performing*. To these, others have added a fifth – *mourning*, to refer to the ending stage.

Forming

CASE STUDY

It is the first session of a group for the parents of school refusers. The facilitator opens with a brief statement setting out the times of meeting and reminding the group that its purpose is to allow members to gain something from the opportunity to meet and share ideas with others who are experiencing a similar problem. This is followed by a long silence, which is broken eventually by two members having an extended discussion about the condition of the school car park. They are interrupted by a third member who talks to the therapist about her child as if no one else is in the room. Finally, one of the first two asks the facilitator what qualifications one needs to run a group like this. Throughout, the other five members stay completely silent.

COMMENT

> *None of these responses to the opening stages of a group is unusual. In the beginning stages, individuals may be frightened or nervous, unsure of what is going to happen or of how they are expected to behave. In the first session, you should expect levels of tension to be high. People will react to this tension in many different ways.*

At this stage the facilitator's task is to help members feel safe and to come together to form a group that is attractive to them. The first group session is of crucial importance. Look back at Chapter 3 on facilitation and particularly at the section on valuing emotion (see page 53). Remind yourself of the basic human needs to love and be loved, to choose and be chosen, and to understand and be understood. When we join a group, we are liable to have (if not to present) anxieties driven by these three pairs of needs.

- **Acceptance anxieties** – Will I be liked, wanted or rejected, or will I be disliked, unwanted or rejected?

- **Orientation anxieties** – Will I understand or make sense; and can I find my identity in the group?

- **Performance anxieties** – Will I be competent and be able to have control or personal power here?

On the surface, these anxieties may be felt through having butterflies, or an increased pulse rate or temperature, or breathing changes in turn translated into nervousness when speaking. One of the authors (Sue) is aware that she has a tendency to speak faster when she is nervous, so brings this to her awareness before facilitating the start of a new group.

Planning the first session
You know how important first impressions can be. This also applies in groupwork. Benson (2001) suggests three simple ideas that are important to get across in the first session.

First, the worker should show that they are competent. The effort that has gone into planning the group should give the members some sense of this, but an open, honest disposition will also help. There is absolutely nothing wrong in confessing to 'first-night nerves'. You can be sure that the members are also feeling apprehensive and there are advantages in modelling the willingness to express vulnerability, even at this early stage. If you can show it, others will feel safer about showing it themselves later. However, you must simultaneously show that, even if nervous, you are not incapacitated or overwhelmed.

Second, you must communicate commitment. You must show that you believe in what you are doing (if you do not, then you need to get out now), that it works and that you will do all in your power to make the project a success.

Third, you should communicate compassion, similar to the supportive intervention in facilitation skills. This can be done as simply as being sure that everybody understands and agrees with what is going on, that it is important to you that they do understand, and that you want to know and be involved with each individual.

As is the case with any piece of work that you do, you need to spend some time preparing yourself for the task ahead. 'Tuning in' is a familiar concept in social work and the same concept applies here. You need to tune in to yourself, what you are feeling, and what your strengths and weaknesses are; you need to tune in to the group members, their hopes, anxieties, concerns, and to the situation itself.

Schwartz (1971) suggests that the essential tasks for groupworkers in the first session are:

• to make a clear and jargon-free statement of the group purpose;

• to describe the role of the facilitator(s) in simple terms;

• *to reach for feedback*, that is, as regards whether they consider that the stated purpose of the group coincides with their own;

• to help the group reach a consensus on the purpose of the group and their frame of reference for being together, including the contract. We have dealt with this in Chapter 4, at least in terms of contracts with individual members. The early sessions of the group provide the opportunity to translate these individual contracts into an overall contract for the whole group.

To these Brown (1992) adds:

• to begin to create a group culture, for example in relation to mutual help and an atmosphere of relative security and trust.

Button (1997) suggests the following to create safety in the group.

• Explain and develop the ground rules. This includes the practical elements, such as knowing where toilets are, through to issues of confidentiality and a clear understanding of the purpose of the group. How much power do participants have; can they decide breaks and renegotiate ground rules? You need to be very clear about these issues before you begin.

• Encourage participation and the active acceptance or rejection of suggestions. To gain useful insights and meaningful learning from a group, participants need to feel safe and protected and be prepared to take risks. This is about offering real, clear achievable choices and making it plain that choosing not to risk is as valid and empowering as choosing to risk, even when you and sometimes the rest of the group believe that the greater gain would come from taking the risk.

ACTIVITY 5.2

Thinking once more about your imaginary group, write down a list of how you think the individuals in the group might behave in the first session. Try to anticipate as many behavioural outcomes as possible, but do not be rigid about it. Consider how to acknowledge and what to do in response.

> ### COMMENT
>
> *It is quite difficult to predict how a group will behave at any given time. However, at the start, the following are not unusual:*
>
> - *members are fearful or unwilling to participate;*
> - *one or two members are very active and dominate the session;*
> - *it is hard to keep the group focused; people ramble and get off the point;*
> - *members are surprisingly compliant and go along with whatever is suggested by the facilitator;*
> - *there are long silences;*
> - *anger or aggression is expressed;*
> - *members ignore each other and relate only to you.*

Storming

As people begin to feel a little more comfortable and self-assured in the group, members start to seek individual roles and space. There can be jostling for positions of power in the group. Testing out takes place while people make judgements about whether the group is likely to be of value to individuals. The facilitators frequently come under serious attack and you need to understand that, although difficult, this is a normal part of group development and does not reflect on you personally. (At the same time, however, there may be very good reasons why you are being challenged, which are nothing to do with 'storming'; that is to say, it does reflect upon you personally!) At a task level, there may be uncertainty about what can be achieved. At this stage, it is important for you, as a facilitator, to know why you are doing what you are doing. This is not in a textbook type of way, but more in the here-and-now, in-this-situation way. Button (1997, p9) offers a couple of good examples of thoughts:

> I am introducing the idea of revenge now because it might help Tom understand his feelings towards his mother.' 'I am not passing the box of tissues to Sophie because it might interrupt her emotional release.'

To help with the storming, sometimes it can be useful to make sure that there is plenty of group activity in which everyone can get involved and that people experience success in what they do. Positive feedback is very helpful at this stage. Easy, safe, but interesting games and exercises are useful in creating this sense of achievement.

Norming

Having explored and tested out roles, and having resolved issues of power and questions about the value of the group, members begin to get a sense of what is required, and rules and norms become established. These can be either positive or negative in terms of the group's objectives, and facilitators have a role in ensuring that norms that develop are constructive. Scapegoating can occur or people can start to lose touch a little with the real world. Programme design should emphasise the links between what is happening in the group and in life outside. Homework exercises or role-plays of problem situations encountered by group members can help.

Performing

Members are now readily cooperating and contributing to the group tasks; the aims of the group are being lived in the life and processes of the group, and the influence of the group on individuals is high. The group is a largely self-sufficient resource, using all the skills and potential of the members to solve its problems. Facilitators may well be able to increase group democracy and some facilitators may find it hard to let go. Many groups do not reach this stage.

Mourning

Members may experience a sense of loss of valued support, feedback and opportunity for personal development when a group ends. They may react in a number of different ways: the group may revert to earlier behaviours; there may be euphoria about what has been achieved; there may be frustration about what has not been achieved.

CASE STUDY

It is the last session of a group programme for women, where the aim was to increase assertiveness. The programme has followed a structure of exercises and has been judged by all to have been a great success. In this last session, two of the group members keep referring to this success and argue that the group should continue for a further two weeks. They use the strategies they have learned in the group, in a humorous way, to reinforce their arguments. The facilitators are somewhat convinced by their arguments and are wondering if they should concede.

COMMENT

Frequently, members want to postpone the end by having additional sessions or reunions. You too will feel tempted to agree, but you should be cautious. It is nearly always best to end the group when planned: additional sessions and reunions can result in poor attendance and an accompanying sense of considerable anticlimax.

To ensure that the group ends successfully, the facilitator(s) should make sure that the end is properly acknowledged and should provide a structure to enable this to happen. Here are some suggestions.

- **Keeping the end in sight** – Make sure that group members are aware of the limited life of the group right from the start and keep reminding them at intervals.

- **Reviewing** – At the end, review what the group has done, and what it has experienced – and within that review what each individual has experienced and contributed.

- **Evaluating** – Following on from the review, evaluate what the group and its members have achieved, especially in relation to the original aims of the group. Remember, too, that this is an opportunity to evaluate the performance of the workers and the success of the programme. We look at evaluation in more detail in Chapter 9.

- **Ending relationships** – You will need to provide an opportunity for members to say 'goodbye' and to deal with any 'unfinished business' between individuals, whether members or facilitators.

- **Preparation for the post-group stage** – As people leave the group, they may need alternative sources of support/action/contact, and the group can help each member to plan accordingly. What resources can the person access? Do you need to have a reintro-duction to his or her individual social worker?

- **Ending rituals** – Some event or happening to mark the ending of a group is often very helpful. This might be some special group exercise, a social occasion, such as a special meal or party, or some creative activity devised by group members.

As we noted earlier, Tuckman's model assumes a linear or sequential progression of group development. Groups do not, in reality, move sequentially through neat phases, but also move in what sometimes seems to be a chaotic fashion backwards and sidewise as well as forwards. Poole (1981) found that group development is often more complicated than Tuckman's model indicates. He argued that groups jump back and forth between three tracks: *task*, *topic* and *relation*. The three tracks can be compared to the intertwined strands of a rope. The *task* track is to do with the processes the group engages in to attain its goals. The *topic* track concerns the specific item the group is discussing at the time. The *relation* track deals with the interpersonal relationships between the group members. At times, the group may stop its work on the task and deal with interpersonal relationships instead. When the group reaches consensus on all three tracks at once, it can develop in a more unified manner.

Schutz (1958) offers an alternative, cyclical model with three stages: *inclusion*, *control* and *affection*. During the *inclusion* phase, members are primarily concerned with whether or not the group will accept them. To reduce the anxiety caused by this, members will share harmless information about themselves, and will chat and make jokes. The group at this stage is characterised by restlessness, tension and mobility. Once these issues are resolved, *control* issues become more important. The group begins to be concerned about issues of power, status, influence, decision-making and communication. An *affection* stage follows that is about participants building emotional ties and deciding on the degree of intimacy to be developed with other members. Clearly, these stages of development are similar to Tuckman's. However, in Schutz's model, since the levels of intimacy in the affection stage differ between members, some members feel isolated from others and so the group has to enter a new stage of inclusion to deal with this; thus, the group moves to more and more sophisticated stages and the model becomes cyclical rather than linear.

Of course, stage models simply provide us with no more than a guide. Every group is different and every group moves through these stages at different rates, with different levels of success and to varying extents. Nevertheless, these models do help us in our work with groups. Brown (1992) reminds us that group process as a concept applies not only to the group over its lifetime but also to each and every session. On each occasion it meets, there is a discernible beginning, middle and end. Knowledge of group development theory helps us in deciding our programme for the group – what exercises or activities might be appropriate at what time and what facilitation behaviours are likely to be the most effective.

Challenges of facilitating groupwork process

Process issues, if unseen or denied, perpetuate inequality and deny access or a voice to certain people. Issues relating to gender, race and ethnicity have all been key influences in the development of groupwork theory and practice in UK social work, largely as a result of wider concerns for anti-discriminatory and anti-oppressive practices, and then with the diversity agenda (Cohen and Mullender, 2003). It has been recognised in recent years that issues of race, gender and ethnicity are much more complex, and there is a need to recognise and embrace the concept of *intersectionality* – the overlap and interaction of oppressions (Gutierrez and Lewis, 1999, cited in Lewis and Gutierrez, 2003). This means, for example, that in the lives of women of colour there is no way for women to separate the issues of ethnicity and gender, and so the interaction between the membership of these two groups is more than, and different from, either one alone. A woman of colour will therefore have experiences and issues that are a combination of her ethnicity and gender. Gender inequalities are the most universal. Mullender (2003, p201) concludes that the issue of gender is relevant in every groupwork context and suggests:

> *in any setting where men or women or both, facilitate groups of men or women or both – that is in all groups – gender issues will arise and the workers need to be sufficiently alert and skilled to deal with them.*

Identifying process issues

In understanding and learning to identify and facilitate process, therefore, it becomes even more important that we develop our self-awareness within all of our zones, and acknowledge and understand the impact of our own gender, identity and communication styles, personality and learning preferences. Remember that we are likely to find it hard to 'see' or 'feel' process issues if we have grown up within the dominant culture or discourse and have never challenged our own assumptions.

CASE STUDY

Mukti gave Stephen a course book written using the pronoun 'she' instead of the more usual 'he'. He returned the book some days later and was amazed that he had not seen how excluding the use of 'he' must be to women. 'I felt that the use of "she" really excluded me from the book; that must happen to you all the time?'

When a process issue emerges in a group, not everyone will be able to identify it immediately, as it takes awareness and practice. When one of the authors (Sue) was training in facilitation, the identification and naming of 'process' issues was one of the most challenging areas of the course. There are several reasons for this. One is because you often 'feel' a process issue before you are able to identify it, and you have to get used to identifying these 'feeling' clues. Sometimes, all you get is a hunch or sense and not a clear understanding of 'it'. All you may be able to say is 'I'm uncomfortable about what is happening' or 'I don't know what it is but something is alerting my feelings.' In a society that often demands that we are articulate and coherent immediately, this is difficult. Button (1997) suggests being prepared to show you are human and make mistakes as one of the elements in creating safety in a group. It can be difficult because of the potential embarrassment of getting it wrong in front of a whole group. He suggests making it easier on yourself by not pretending to be all-wise, all-knowing and superhuman.

Another reason is that, by identifying a hidden issue, we may be confronting a difficult area for the group and being in the presence of the whole group magnifies all the anxieties we experience when confronting one individual. (See the confrontation intervention in Chapter 3, page 54.) You can take some comfort from the fact that, when you experience real fear in anticipation of identifying a process issue, many other group members may silently feel the same fear. Subsequent naming of the fear is often greeted with universal relief.

Yet another reason why facilitating process is tricky is that, when new to groupwork, your own process feelings and experiences can take over and swamp you. This makes it difficult to have 'attention out of the group', which enables you to observe what is happening. With experience, you will learn to trust and use your own process responses, and be more able to use the information they give you to inform your facilitation and choice of intervention.

ACTIVITY *5.3*

Read these examples taken from the books cited. Identify the process issues and then what was done to address them in each. Discuss these examples with colleagues. Do you have other ideas to address the process issues?

> It was very difficult for some women to speak out and very difficult for others to shut up. We had to learn to share conversations: we asked another woman to speak before we did, noisy women partnered up with quieter women, we played the five bean game (where you start with five beans and give one up each time you speak, so no one has more than five turns), and we used picture language and signs to help women without words to join in.
>
> *(The Members of Women First, 2003, p118)*

> The opening ritual consisted of reading the mission of the organisation, 'to create a safe and supportive environment for gay, lesbian, bi, trans and questioning youth,' followed by a reading of the ground rules. A large laminated copy of the ground rules was passed from hand to hand and each person read one of the rules aloud. 'No side conversations.' . . . 'What is said in the meeting stays in the meeting.' . . . 'No shame blame or guilt.'
>
> *(DeLois, 2003, p108)*

87

> **COMMENT**
>
> *In both these examples, the groups devised 'activities' to help them illuminate and improve the processes. The five bean exercise raised awareness of how many times people spoke in the group and helped others to monitor this; reading from and passing round the large illuminated copy of the ground rules gave value to the rules and reinforced them at the start of each session.*

Learning and being assessed in groups

Here, before finishing this chapter, we take a slight detour and consider the challenges faced by you as a student when you are learning and being assessed in groups. This section should be useful for you not only in furthering your understanding of the concepts we have just considered, but also in helping you to be a successful learner in group situations. As a successful learner you will increase your knowledge and skills, but also with a better understanding of process you should also score more highly when you are being assessed as a member of a group.

In Chapter 1 we looked at the ways in which learning could be enhanced through groups as identified by Jaques (2000). There are also a number of advantages of assessment in groups: where learning is taking place in groups, group assessment provides continuity between learning and assessment; it offers opportunities to assess skills such as team work, communication, collaboration and project management; and it may be time-saving, or at least more interesting, than other assessment methods for teachers and lecturers. There are, of course, a number of potential disadvantages: it can be difficult to evaluate the contribution of each individual (although this may be achieved, for example by setting individual tasks within the group task, or tasks in addition to the group task, or by including elements of peer- and/or self-assessment in order to individualise a mark awarded for the whole group); there is a tendency to assess the outcome, for example a group presentation, rather than the process of the group interaction and learning; and it can be subjective. It is highly improbable that you will proceed through your course without, at least, experiencing learning in groups and it is also very likely that you will experience being assessed in a group. How do you make the most of these situations? First, we would say that you need to realise that it is the performance of the group, acting as a group, that will make for a helpful experience. Approaching the task as a self-interested individual will be counterproductive. Your effort needs to be directed towards the good of the group. Only in this way will you derive benefit from your own effort. If the group wins, everybody wins. This is where an understanding of process becomes important. Let us return, therefore, and look in greater detail at some of the processes that may be particularly helpful to you as identified by Douglas (1995) and cited earlier in this chapter.

Interaction is a two-way street: potentially it can have either a positive or negative effect on the group as a whole and on individual members. The quality of interaction is an important factor in determining the level of understanding, the spread of information, opinions adopted, strengthened or confirmed, and, importantly for our discussion here, the level of achievement. Douglas (1995) suggests a number of important factors influencing interaction:

- being aware of others in close proximity;

- being frequently exposed to others;

- the level of intensity of the exposure;

- the need to have approved behaviour reinforced;

- the personality of the individuals, for example in terms of extraversion/introversion;

- the previous experience of members;

- the perceptions members have of each other, for example in terms of similarity, status or attractiveness;

- the need for resources and support;

- the quality of communication.

Communication: when it comes to thinking about how the group can communicate more effectively, it may be useful to focus on your own skills, rather than those of the people around you. You will communicate more effectively when you:

- listen to everyone, even when you are bursting to speak;

- observe others;

- participate, even if only non-verbally;

- say what is on your mind, even if you are not totally sure you are right (but not if you repeat it endlessly);

- are sensitive, both to others and to yourself and how you affect others;

- let others have their say – don't interrupt and don't hog the limelight;

- try to ensure that everyone has a chance, or, better, is encouraged to contribute;

- seek clarification when you don't understand;

- stick to the task and encourage others to do the same;

- are not competitive but, nevertheless, are assertive;

- develop ideas, including those that are not your own;

- do not introduce irrelevant material;

- check that you are clear about what has been decided.

The ability of others to communicate well will be adversely affected when:

- they feel they cannot express themselves well;

- they fear ridicule or hostility;

- they feel left out or marginalised;

- they feel their comments are resented, even when valid;

- they are inattentive.

Communication in the group generally will not be good if the group:

- makes restrictive rules that block the flow of communication, for example people can only speak when it's their turn;

- gets stuck on one topic, especially if it is either irrelevant or not going anywhere;

- gets stuck on detail and minutiae.

Decision-making: when learning in a group you will be faced with many decisions that the group needs to take. When the group is being formally assessed, decision-making will be crucial – for example, what topic to present, what form a report should take, or how roles and tasks are to be allocated.

We saw in Chapter 2 how factors such as group size, frequency of contact, intensity, composition, etc. make a difference in how a group functions. These *structural* factors consequently will be of importance in determining how easily the group can make satisfactory and effective decisions. However, it will also be helpful to consider other factors, some of which may have already occurred to you from discussion in this or earlier chapters.

- **The stage of group development** – Tuckman (see page 80) would argue that the group needs to have reached the *performing* stage before being able to make decisions effectively. For this reason, you may find it difficult to make lasting satisfactory decisions early in the group's life. Just as you need to read around a subject for a while before committing yourself to paper in a written assignment, it may save time in the long run to spend time getting to know other members of your group before making major decisions about the assessment task.

- **The nature of the task** – Deliberately spend time with the other members of the group, ensuring that you have a common and accurate understanding of the task.

- **How decisions are to be reached** – Is this by consensus? How and in what circumstances can dissension be accommodated – majority vote?

- **Whether there are to be any rules and sanctions** – for example, for freeloaders. How will you deal with people who do not contribute fairly?

- **How you are going to tackle the task before you start**.

- **Whether it is possible for the task to be divided** – As a group, do you wish to allocate sub-tasks to individuals or sub-groups?

- **Pressure** – Inevitably you will face increasing pressure as the deadline approaches. What can you do in the early stages to forestall this? Can you agree a schedule of activity? Can you afford the time to draw this up?

CHAPTER SUMMARY

- It is important to be able to distinguish between content and process in groups – between the *what* and the *how* in a group – because, as we saw in Chapter 3, we need to be able to understand what is happening in the group at the individual, interpersonal and whole-group levels.

- When we are able to recognise what is happening in terms of group process, then we are able to work with it and also to influence it.

- Processes in groups follow predictable patterns and themes; this has allowed theorists to develop models of group development. This is very useful to us as facilitators as we can take account of it in our planning, not only in relation to the programme for the life of the group, but also in relation to each session.

- Understanding process can result in you achieving more when you are a learner in a group and can help the group achieve a better outcome when being assessed as a group.

FURTHER READING

Benson, J (2001) *Working More Creatively with Groups*, 2nd edition. London: Routledge.

This text has an excellent section on process. It includes Benson's theory of love/will polarities and useful advice on how to facilitate the group in its journey through different stages.

Brown, A (1992) *Groupwork*, 3rd edition. Aldershot: Arena.

There is a chapter in this book in which Brown provides useful summaries of the stages models developed by Tuckman and Schutz, along with suggestions for associated facilitator behaviour.

Douglas, T (1995) *Survival in Groups: The basics for group membership*. Buckingham: Open University Press.

This is a valuable resource. While it is written to help people survive as group members, it contains very useful material for group facilitators, especially with regard to process.

Whitaker, DS (2001) *Using Groups to Help People*, 2nd edition. Hove: Brunner-Routledge.

Here you will be able to find Whitaker's group focal conflict theory. She also has a chapter on developmental stages, which includes some discussion of related problems and their solutions.

Chapter 6
Programming and activities

Introduction

In the last chapter we looked at the concept of process in groups, how patterns and themes that arise in group process allow us to make predictions about how a group is likely to change over time, and how we can use this knowledge in deciding what we should be doing with a group as it changes and develops. In this chapter we are going to take these ideas a little further and think about programming and activities. Group activities are simply the things that we plan that the group will do. These can be exercises or games, discussions, talks by guest speakers, videos, trips or even just having a cup of tea together. A programme is a thought-out sequential list of these activities, not dissimilar really from the sort of programme you might find for a week's television or radio.

Vinter (1967, p95) helps us to understand what we mean by *programme* in the context of groupwork. He explains that it does not *refer to all the social interactions and processes engaged in by group* members but denotes:

> *a general class of group activities, each of which consists of an interconnected, sequential series of social behaviours. [They] tend to follow a more-or-less typical pattern, unfolding in a rough chronological sequence, and, for some, reaching a definite climax or conclusion.*

A programme, therefore, is a series of group activities, planned in a logical order to meet the aims of the group. We suggested earlier that it is not a good idea to plan your group in too much detail at the beginning, as you may need to allow for things that happen (group processes) as you go along. Nevertheless, you will need to have, at least, a general plan of what will happen throughout the lifetime of the group. Even the sort of groups that Rogers (1970) describes – those on the unstructured end of Burnard's (1990) spectrum (see Chapter 3, page 56) – require a programme plan, if only so that the group can start and finish satisfactorily. We need to have a general plan for the duration of the group and then more detailed plans for each session as it comes up.

Programming

Programming brings with it certain advantages.

- It provides a focus for people to come together and a context in which they can interact.

- It provides structure for the group. A structured experience provides group members with certainty and security. It helps them feel safer and they are able to predict what is going to happen next and in the future in the group. As Benson (2001) points out, *Context creates boundaries and boundaries create rules and structure, consistency and predictability* (p31).

- It provides a reason in itself for attending the group. This can be for both the individual and her or his friends and families. Sometimes people may feel embarrassed about attendance or be put under pressure from significant people in their lives *not* to attend. The programme can provide arguments for attending: 'I've got to go every night'; 'I've got to go tonight; it's about welfare benefits.'

- The programme may facilitate the growth and development of the group. We saw in Chapter 5 that the concept of *process* is important in groups and that groups typically go through *stages of development*. Since, to some extent, we can predict the development of the group, we can plan to take account of this in the programme planning; we can choose activities that will help the group to move through these stages or that will influence the processes in the group in ways that are beneficial. So, for example, we are able to make sure that we start with safe activities that help each individual's confidence; slightly later, we may have a focus on developing a trusting atmosphere; later still, we may include activities that help with self-disclosure, and so on.

We need to acknowledge, at this point, that 'off-the-shelf' programmes have become increasingly common. Sometimes this is due to the lack of the time, resources or even expertise needed to plan a programme from scratch. Partly, it has come about as a result of an 'outcome culture', which demands named, measurable and accredited programmes rather than those that allow a more bespoke, process-driven approach. Often it is because evaluations have demonstrated that a particular programme is very effective. Examples include *Respect*, a national programme for working with domestic violence perpetrators, the facilitation of which is reviewed by Blacklock (2003); and *Journey to Freedom*, a programme used by Women's Aid that focuses on raising survivors' awareness of a number of related issues, such as myths surrounding domestic violence, the impact on the children and the typical profile of the abuser.

It may be that these 'off-the-shelf' courses or manuals are applicable to your group and they may be worth considering rather than designing your own. However, as Doel (2006) points out, *the advantages of having a ready-tested format has to be balanced against the possibility of having to squeeze* this *group into* that *manual* (p49; our emphasis).

RESEARCH SUMMARY

By the early 1990s a body of research involving meta-analysis of a large number of groupwork programmes (for example, Andrews et al., 1990; Lipsey, 1992) concluded that work with offenders that was effective in reducing offending had a number of significant characteristics, one of which was 'programme integrity'. This principle means that programmes should be delivered as planned, that is, that the groupworkers should not vary from the 'script'.

The principle of programme integrity presents a number of difficulties. First, it can result in workers following the programme in a mechanical way. Second, staff may be required to run programmes about which they lack enthusiasm or to which they are not committed, resulting in a lack of confidence in the programme on the part of the members. Third, it can be difficult to accommodate and respond appropriately to group processes. Fourth, there is little opportunity to consult with the members on the programme content. Finally, it is difficult to tailor a standardised programme to the needs of the individual or group. Barry (2006, p185) makes the point succinctly:

> *Irrespective of them (standardised programmes) often being inappropriate to . . . people's intellectual and maturational capacities, such group-oriented programmes by definition also restrict the adoption of an holistic and tailor made approach to . . . people's problems.*

We recognise that a sound grasp of groupwork knowledge and skills is essential when facilitating these set programmes and we do not have a problem with 'off-the-shelf' group programmes per se. Our difficulty is that, when they are delivered in a rigid and inflexible way, no account can be taken of the actual profile of the group, the characteristics and individual needs of the members, nor of the processes that take place. As Blacklock (2003, cited in Preston-Shoot, 2007) suggests, in facilitating standardised programmes we need to take care to ensure that we do what we can to support, carry through and make sense of the activities that they contain and not simply deliver them in a mechanical way.

Thinking through how you might design and structure a programme

It is not possible to embark on planning a programme of activities for a group without having a very clear idea of what is the aim of the group and the intended outcome. The intended outcome will determine the type of group that you are hoping to plan. Wilson et al. (2000, cited in DeLucia-Waack and Nitza, 2013) classify three types of small helping groups: psychoeducational, counselling and therapy groups.

- **Psychoeducational groups** have a focus on learning, in terms of both the acquisition of knowledge and the development and/or enhancement of skills. Interventions are aimed at helping members to share and develop better ways of coping with new or challenging situations and can be either at the level of thinking, feeling or behaving, or a combination of these. Anger management, social skills, stress management, problem solving and assertiveness training groups are all examples of this approach.

- **Counselling groups** may include elements of education and skill development but are more concerned with using the relationships that develop in the group to promote positive change – with the interactions, mutual sharing and emotional growth. The facilitator's role is in helping the members to understand how relations are developing, or otherwise, and what is happening in the group, in fact the group processes. As with individual psychotherapy, change occurs as a result of what happens 'in the room'. There is an assumption, however, that the members will bring into the group relationship behaviours from their outside world. The group can then examine these behaviours and provide feedback. New positive relationship patterns brought about through this process can then be exported into the 'real' life outside. Particular facilitator skills are the same as in individual counselling – reflection, active listening, clarification, summarising etc. Groups for people with relationship problems are examples of counselling groups.

- **Therapy groups** *address personal and interpersonal problems of living, remedial perceptual and cognitive distortions or repetitive patterns of dysfunctional behavior* (Wilson et al., 2000, cited in DeLucia-Waack and Nitza, 2013). Although therapy groups may include skill development, for example refusal skills, and are also concerned with process, the focus here is more on helping with problems that are severe or chronic. Examples might be people with substance misuse problems, sex offenders, domestic violence perpetrators and also their victims and other people with repetitive and dysfunctional patterns of interacting, thinking and behaving. Cognitive approaches are often common, such as Rational Emotive Behaviour Therapy (see Lindsay, 2013).

We saw earlier in the chapter that we can take account of what we know about group development in devising our programme. In programming you need to be thinking in terms of processes that may happen in each session, as well as programming over the lifespan of the group. In Chapter 3 we introduced the six categories of intervention (Heron, 1989), namely supportive, catalytic (encouraging self-directed learning) and cathartic (valuing emotion), and informative, confronting (pointing out behaviour that is restrictive for the person or the group) and prescriptive. Figure 6.1 provides a suggested order of interventions for a session. Having some guidance to help you decide when to do what when planning a session can be helpful, especially in answering questions such as 'When would it be best to put the most challenging exercise?' or 'How do I make sure we have time for insight and digestion of exercises?' Consideration of timing, intention and the purpose of activities and

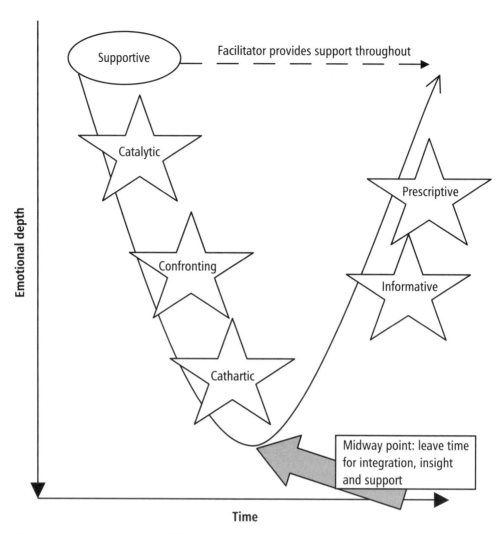

Figure 6.1: Suggested order of interventions

where these are best placed in the session (or programme) is vital, especially if your programme is aiming to enable self-development and to encourage opportunities for self-awareness and insight. If you follow this shape you will not fall into the trap of putting a powerful and challenging exercise too close to the end of a session, leaving the participants (and you) with no time to process the exercise, give value to any emotional responses, gain insights and prepare to leave and return to life outside the group.

The figure shows the order in which you might employ the six categories of intervention. Notice how the line curves; this is to represent how the emotional intensity deepens as the group progresses towards its midway point, and then how the intensity needs to ease off as the group reaches its conclusion.

1. **Supportive** – At all times throughout an activity, session and programme your intention should be to be supportive, affirming the worth and value of all the individuals in the group, including their qualities, attitudes or actions. Each session begins with an intention

to be supportive by making space for some connection or reconnection with individuals and with the intention and aims of the group. DeLois (2003, p108), cited in Chapter 5, offers an example of a supportive beginning (see page 87).

2. **Catalytic, confronting and cathartic** – For the purposes of the illustration, these interventions are depicted as coming one after the other, but they need not necessarily do so. You may need to confront the group in order to encourage self-awareness (catalytic). The point is that they need to come at an earlier stage – we are suggesting before the midway point – so as to allow time for consolidation and recovery. This gives time for any emotional response, release and insights to be digested, and then allows you and the group to gather information and ideas, and to plan for assimilating the lessons learnt outside the group.

3. **Informative and prescriptive** – We have placed these after the midway point, at a time when the level of emotional intensity is waning.

The figure is intended only for general guidance but provides a helpful framework for planning activities to make the best of your group time. Following the shape does not mean that you must not confront someone just before a group ends, for example to challenge a discriminatory remark, but be mindful of the consequences (very little time to process the intervention) of your timing.

Another body of knowledge that is useful is designing learning. One of the most effective ways to learn is through our own experience and the term *experiential learning* describes the type of learning that we do through active and aware involvement of body, mind, emotion, intuition and spirit. Most learning that takes place in groups tends to be experiential. Experiential learning is challenging to facilitate and yet it can be the most rewarding because you are working *with* people and aiming to provide them with experiences and opportunities to take responsibility for their own circumstances, and build on their learning within a supportive environment. This is the *constructivist* approach (see Parton and O'Byrne, 2000). When we learn something, we are likely to experience and notice what we are doing, then think about or reflect on that experience; we may then revise and test our experience before deciding on a general principle of behaviour. (We expect you will be familiar with these ideas from Kolb's (1984) Learning Circle, where these stages are referred to as *concrete experience*, *reflective observation*, *abstract conceptualisation* and *active experimentation*. If you are not, see Parker (2004, p30). People have different personal learning styles (see Parker, 2004, p48). We have a tendency to design interventions or activities for learning in accordance with our own preferences, and we may fail to realise the need to provide exercises or approaches to suit other ways of learning. Bear this in mind when you are thinking about activities and exercises for your groupwork projects.

Some potential pitfalls

Generally speaking, putting a programme together should be relatively straightforward, so long as we are careful to keep a number of points in mind. Benson (2001) suggests a number of common mistakes in programming. These are:

- failure to base the programme on the unmet needs identified originally;

- failure to base the programme on the group aims and objectives;

- failure to make sense of the programme for the participants; the programme is taking place but no connection is made between what is happening and how it relates to the goals;

- failure to allow sufficient space in the programme to take account of unexpected events and opportunities;

- the programme is too repetitive, unimaginative or under-stimulating, so that people become jaded and bored;

- the programme gives the appearance of industry, but in fact no real work is taking place; the group is static, a phenomenon sometimes referred to as *dynamic inertia*;

- the programme is planned, but the facilitators do not review and evaluate it, and so fail to fine-tune it or redesign it.

To these we would add the following.

- Over-programming – planning too much can also be unhelpful. Doel (2006, p115) suggests that over-programming can lead group members to behave as passengers, since the responsibility for the group is never theirs.

- The programme becomes an end in itself. We should always remember that a programme of activity is only a means of helping us to achieve the aims of the group. It is not an end in itself and we should not allow it to stand in our way in reaching our goal. Sometimes we may forget this and think that the programme is the most important thing – we are determined to finish this part of the programme on time so that the next activity can take place as scheduled. We ignore the fact that we can make much better use of something that is happening *here and now*, but that at first appears to be disrupting the group programme.

CASE STUDY

In a programme for a parenting skills group, the sixth session was to focus on ways of managing difficult behaviour. The facilitators had decided to start with getting the members to call out situations where a child's behaviour was difficult to control. This was to be followed by showing a DVD that would give guidance on managing difficult behaviour. A guest speaker was then to arrive and provide information on behaviour-control techniques. During the first part of the session, a group member referred repeatedly to a newspaper item about a child who had been abducted and then returned a day later. The facilitators, aware that they had a DVD to show before the arrival of the expert, pushed on relentlessly. During the expert's session, the group member referred to the newspaper item yet again. The expert allowed the conversation to develop. The parent who had raised the item talked about how frightened the child must have been, recounting an experience when they themselves had been left in a children's play area at a carpet warehouse; another described having been lost at an air display for over two hours. Someone else spoke of being left in the care of a stranger when very little. This led to a discussion of child neglect and how people who had been neglected might find it difficult to provide good parenting. These were all themes that the facilitators were able to return to in later sessions, but these opportunities might not have arisen had the programme been followed as planned.

Activities

What activities should we choose? The first thing to bring to mind is that the planned activities in a group should follow logically from the aims and objectives of the group, which themselves derive from the identified unmet needs of the members; this we discussed in Chapter 3:

unmet need → aim/s and objectives → programme → activities.

Any group involves activities. Unstructured discussion is an activity; so is a coffee break or a trip to the cinema. We have seen earlier in this chapter that a programme is a planned sequence of activities. Whitaker (1985) gives seven categories.

- **An activity that is done purely for the fun of doing it** – The activity has in itself no purpose other than enjoyment. Examples might include football, pool, dancing or eating out. However, you should note that almost all activities involve some interaction and therefore can have attendant benefits: for example, people get to know each other; they help with relationships in the group; or they provide material for later discussion.

- **An activity that is designed to generate interaction and can then be used as a basis for helpful intervention later** – One of the authors (Trevor) used to take young people caving; the experience provided opportunities later for discussion about who had been most helpful to others, who had been most adventurous, and who had found the activity easiest (usually the smallest!).

- **An activity that provides an opportunity to rehearse a skill** – Examples might be using role-play to prepare for a job interview or a carer explaining to a dependent relative that he or she will be going into respite care.

- **An activity that is analogous to something else** – The activity provides a way of understanding that other situation or how individuals behave in that situation. One such activity, 'Baby you can drive my car', involves the group members placing themselves around a chair (the driver's seat), each representing a part of the car they see themselves as in the group. Examples might be the brakes (I slow the group down to avoid anyone getting hurt), the accelerator (I speed the group up, progressing discussion), or the fuel tank (I provide the group with energy or ideas). The 'car' provides an analogy for the group and helps members understand how individuals perceive the roles they are playing.

- **An activity that provides an alternative route or perhaps a more certain route to something that could otherwise happen in discussion** – Exercises such as 'What matters' (see 'Example games and exercises', page 104), where members take turns at answering questions written on a pack of index cards, help to generate discussion around a particular topic.

- **An exercise or activity that is an accelerating device, causing something to happen more quickly than it perhaps otherwise would** – Icebreakers, designed to help people more quickly become comfortable with the group experience, fall into this category, as do naming games and trust-building exercises.

- **An activity or exercise that helps members empathise, either with each other, or with people with whom they interact** – A good example is reverse role-play, where someone is asked to take the role of her or his parent, or son or daughter, while someone else in the group, perhaps a facilitator, plays the part of the individual. Social workers in Youth Offending Teams use a number of similar exercises to increase victim empathy.

Different activities generate different types of experience. Activity experiences should be generally rewarding and expected to be particularly helpful to certain service users. However, not all people experience the same activity in the same way. Some activities that are helpful to some may be unhelpful, unrewarding or potentially damaging for others. To be most useful to most people, we should look at activities from the point of view of the experiences that they are likely to generate, and then design them with the needs of certain group members in mind.

Vinter (1967, p97) suggests that all activities have three components. These are:

- **physical field** – the physical space in which the activity takes place and the *social objects* that are characteristic of the activity, for example an open space, a parachute and participants for parachute games, a dining-room table, chairs, crockery, cutlery and diners for a dinner;

- **performance behaviours** – the behaviours that are *required* for the activity taking place, and that are required for participation, for example eating at dinner;

- **respondent behaviours** – those behaviours associated with the activity but that are not essential to it, for example talking and listening at dinner – behaviours *evoked* by the activity.

Vinter explains why this analysis is important. Both these behaviours are brought about by the activity, more or less regardless of the personalities of the participants. It is these behaviours that are essential for the group to achieve its objectives. The behaviours can be modified by the selection or modification of activities. Consequently, we need to be aware of which features of an activity are likely to bring about what behaviours, so that we can produce a programme that will help the group to meet its objectives.

Vinter suggests, therefore, that we need to consider the following dimensions.

- **How prescriptive is the activity?** To what extent does the activity prescribe certain behaviours and thus control the individual's behaviour? How much choice is there for individuals in terms of how they participate? Can they opt out of the whole activity, or part of it? What restrictions does it put on other behaviour? Watching a DVD can be very prescriptive (don't talk or move around, watch the screen), whereas a role-play may be much less so. It is likely that individuals in your group may have different responses to different activities. Some may not wish to participate in an activity at all. It is useful for you to have thought through how you will respond to a refusal to participate, or a challenge about the way an activity is conducted, before you introduce it. It may be worth considering this situation in the discussion and clarification of the ground rules at the very beginning of the group, as we suggested in creating safety in groups (see Chapter 5). Personally, we have found that offering autonomy and freedom of choice to participants, with a suggestion that they quietly reflect on why they are choosing not to take part, is usually a helpful approach. This supports their ability to choose, values defences and can often provide the space for reflection on a difficult issue without avoidance. This approach can provide insight that is then shared in the processing of the exercise. However, we are also conscious of the fact that, in groups where attendance is required, for example by a court, participation is also compulsory, but we have often questioned the usefulness of this.

- **Who or what controls the participants' behaviour within the activity?** Is it a person, as in a referee for football? Is it the rules, as in chess? Alternatively, is it a participant, as in a game of 'Tag' or 'Follow the leader'?

CASE STUDY

In a group for people with mental health problems, the facilitators were using relaxation exercises. One of the group members volunteered that she had done some similar exercises before and suggested bringing them to the next session. The facilitators thought that it was an excellent idea and the next group started with the group member leading the group through a new exercise. This involved the members lying on their backs as they were led through a fantasy in which they imagined themselves rising through levels of a pyramid, at each level being bathed in a different colour, until finally they arrived at the apex of the pyramid, where they were surrounded by a pure white light. Immediately after the exercise, some of the black members of the group said that they experienced the exercise as being racist, in that it supported ideas around white supremacy.

There will be times when it may be entirely appropriate to hand over a leading role to a group member. Indeed, leaders will emerge in the natural course of every group. However, we need to remember that responsibility for the group never leaves the facilitators and, when in the role, we need to do everything possible to ensure the well-being of all the members.

- **How much interaction among group members does the activity require or permit?** What rewards do group members receive, how quickly are they distributed, and how often? Think of rewards in terms of gratification arising from doing something well, getting positive feedback, being praised, feeling more relaxed or more confident, and so on.

- **What level of ability is required?** Are there special skills or levels of fitness/agility/strength needed? Does the activity demand a certain level of intellectual ability? What kind of bodily movement does the activity allow and/or require?

Whitaker (1985) suggests that, before selecting a particular activity for one's group, one should ask oneself a number of additional questions.

- **Whose needs does the activity meet?** It is easy to fall into the trap of using an exercise because you, personally, find it very enjoyable, or perhaps because it will fill some space in the programme that you cannot think how to fill otherwise. In these circumstances, the activity is meeting the needs of the facilitator, rather than the group.

- **What are all the consequences of utilising the device?** This includes both the intended and unintended likely consequences. Unintended consequences can arise for an individual or for the group as a whole. Some exercises rely on the participants not being able to predict what will happen, although the facilitator knows. The surprise is intended to produce some learning. A consequence, however, might be that the group experiences the facilitator as someone who is dishonest and untrustworthy.

- **Are the consequences the same or different for different participants?** For example, will the exercise provide an experience of success for some and of failure for others? Some people take enjoyment out of close physical contact, while others find it most uncomfortable.

CASE STUDY

Two social workers were running a group for young people who had been excluded from school. They felt that it was important that the young people gave each other feedback about their behaviour and used a game to help with this process (see 'The computer game' on page 105). The game involved the group members picking a card from a pack, reading a phrase on the card, such as 'The person I'd most like as my friend' and then giving the card to the person to whom they felt it applied. At the end of the game, all but one of the participants, Celine, had a pile of cards in front of them. Celine had none and was understandably upset.

The social workers had not anticipated this happening. It had not happened before and so they had not been ready to intervene to prevent it on this occasion. Had they been prepared for this they could easily have prevented it happening by giving Celine some cards themselves or by casually mentioning that she did not have any before it was too late.

- **Are any of the likely consequences for the group in general, or for specific persons, likely to be damaging in character?** Competitive games, for example, can cause conflict and splitting in a group, and for some a sense of failure – good reasons, you may think, to avoid them.

- **If damaging, can you modify the device to forestall these difficulties?** Whitaker (1985) argues that, if the answer to the question is 'no', then the device should be discarded.

- **What preparation or follow-up is required in order for the group to achieve potential benefits or avoid damage?** It is generally accepted that, for role-plays for example, participants need to have time to get into role and to get out of it again. Some activities may bring about very strong emotions, so that people need time and space and support to help them recover. Figure 6.1 (see page 96) provides some suggestions for this.

- **In what ways could the activity possibly go wrong?** If it should do so, what action might the facilitator take to avoid or reduce any possible damage? In the example of the above case study involving 'The computer game', a casual remark about the fact that Celine had no cards might have been sufficient to change the situation.

Example games and exercises

A large number of games are to be found in various publications; we list some of these in the recommendations for further reading at the end of the chapter. Here, we wish to mention just a few that we have found particularly useful, partly because of their versatility; they can be adapted for a variety of groups, situations and purposes. The original sources of some of these are unknown; they have been collected and handed down through time from worker to worker. Where we know the original sources we have given them. Variations are to be found in some of the recommended texts, where they appear under a variety of names.

Taking time to get to know each other

Time spent at the start of a group helping and encouraging participants to get to know each other can be invaluable in setting the tone for the whole programme. Think of 'getting to know' activities as a road or path into the content of the programme and make the process gradual and interesting so that, by the end of the activity, everyone knows everyone in the room, including their names, something positive or special about them, and their particular circumstances; they have also discussed how they feel about joining the group, and maybe some hopes and fears. An example is 'Milling and pairing', and it might go something like this.

> 'We are going to begin by getting to know each other. So, get so you can move about the room and just make eye contact with people as you move around. You may feel embarrassed; I usually do, but just go with it, and smile at people as you move around.' . . . 'Now stop in pairs and take time to introduce yourself to each other, and perhaps share something about your journey here.' Leave two to three minutes and remind them to take turns listening and talking: 'Move around again and repeat this with one or two more people', then 'Now find a new person and share something positive about you' (they can be encouraged to help each other if needed). Again, two to three minutes, then 'Now find another new person and talk about this group and what you are expecting from it.' This can usefully be repeated two to three times with slightly different conversations. Finally, 'Last time now, find a pair and discuss your hopes and fears; after a few minutes find another pair and sit down in fours and compare notes.'

This exercise can usefully take 20–40 minutes depending on the size of the group and the 'gradient' of the road you want to provide. You don't need or want to hear any of the conversations that go on during this period, only to manage the process in a firm and supportive manner, moving people round, reminding them to listen and talk in turn (a good way to introduce listening skills) and making sure they mix well.

At the end of an activity like this, the group will be better placed to discuss ground rules and articulate their hopes and fears, because they know each other and will realise that they have much in common. You can build into the later stages of this exercise the beginnings of any content and processes you wish to explore later in the programme.

The truth game

The purpose of this exercise is to promote discussion in the group, usually around a particular topic. One could anticipate that this discussion might take place eventually in any case, but the exercise ensures that it does, and also that everyone has an equal opportunity to contribute.

> The group sits in a circle. One additional chair, cushion, or whatever, is designated 'the Chair'. The members of the group take turns to sit in the Chair and answer a personal question put by each other member in turn. Additional rules can be created – supplementary questions can be asked in addition to the main question; the person in the Chair can refuse to answer any question with which they feel uncomfortable; the person in the Chair can add anything they like at the end.

This exercise is highly adaptable. Depending on the type of group or the situation to be addressed, the questions can be limited to a particular topic, for example: 'your experience as a student on a social work course', 'your use of alcohol', or 'your experience of caring for someone with a disability'. Care needs to be taken to ensure that participants have choice – not to answer, only to disclose what they wish, and not to be harassed or scapegoated.

It is worth noting that the exercise needs to run its full course, so that everyone has an equal turn, and therefore a substantial period of time needs to be allowed for this, perhaps a minimum of 10–15 minutes per person. It is a very powerful demonstration of equal opportunities if you manage the time fairly, so that everyone can take a turn.

What matters

This is another game to facilitate discussion. As far as we are aware, the original form of this was a card game called 'Family matters', produced for use with groups of young people by Marriage Guidance (now Relate) in the late 1970s. It has since been adapted many times for a variety of purposes and, of course, you will be able to create your own version for your own purpose.

> The game comprises a set of cards (50 or more depending on the size of the group; there should be about seven or eight cards per member) on each of which is printed a question or instruction. The cards are dealt out so that each person has about five, the remainder left as a pack on the table. The group members take turns to choose and answer the question on one of their cards. If they do so successfully (to the satisfaction of the other members), they are awarded a score as is also printed on the card. The player returns the card to the bottom of the pack and replaces it with one from the top. The scores on the cards are graded in terms of the self-disclosure involved, so that a question such as 'Describe your favourite place' might rate 5 points, whereas 'What worries you most about sex?' would score 20.

As with 'The truth game', the game can be designed for the particular group or purpose you wish. It has the advantage that the participants have a choice about which of their five questions they answer. The cards should have a good mix in terms of how easy they are to answer. Be prepared for quite emotional responses to what appear to be innocent questions.

> CASE STUDY
>
> *A group of adults were playing 'What matters' to help members start to disclose. One member became very distressed while responding to a card saying 'Describe your house.' The house the member was describing had until recently been the matrimonial home, occupied by a partner who had left. This is not a situation that we should be worried about; people will respond to games and exercises at the level that is comfortable for them. However, we do need to be aware that people may react in ways that we do not expect.*

The computer game

The purpose of this game is to help people to give and receive feedback. (Remember the Johari window in Figure 3.1 on page 50.)

> The game is based on a set of cards on each of which is a descriptive statement – for example, 'The person I would like as a friend'; 'The person who always seems to get a rough deal'; or 'The person who works hardest'. Some skill is required in designing a set of statements that vary in terms of intimacy and that are appropriately challenging and supportive, but not damaging. The cards are placed on a table and participants take turns to read out a card and allocate it to whom they think appropriate.

With this activity it is important to give people plenty of choice; thus, rules can be added, allowing people to choose a different card, to allocate cards to themselves and to refuse to accept a card that they feel does not apply to them.

In the case of each of these games, you can follow the exercise with a less structured discussion of the issues raised.

Questionnaires

We have used questionnaires mostly to help members get to know each other at the beginning of a group. Different versions exist. A basic version is a list of statements about individuals in the group – for example, 'The person who lives in Anytown'; or 'The person who works in a shoe shop'. Members are required to complete the questionnaire by going around the group finding out to whom each statement applies. Questions can be designed around the characteristics of the actual group members (remembering to have an equal number of questions for each individual), or can be more general – for example, 'A person wearing blue jeans'; or 'A person who can swim'. Care needs to be taken not to stereotype people or to include questions that might be offensive, such as those that refer to physical characteristics – height, weight, age – or those that highlight ethnic difference; 'A person with brown eyes' might apply primarily to black and Asian people in the group, for example.

Versions of this include cards made out like bingo cards, so that people can call 'LINE' or 'HOUSE', when they are the first to complete these. (Yes, we realise that this introduces competition, but it is a matter of judgement as to whether anyone is likely consequently to experience failure. If so, do not use the exercise in this form.)

We now bring in the third part of the Group Planner.

Group Planner

Part three: the programme

What topics, games and/or activities are to be used?

What are the potential benefits of these?

Are they the same for everyone?

What are the hazards?

What can I do to forestall these?

Are the activities appropriate, given the composition of the group in terms of mix of gender, ethnicity, ability and other characteristics?

In what order should I/we use them, taking into account group development?

COMMENT

Although there are fewer questions in this part of the Planner, the answers are probably longer. Remember that, if you plan the whole programme in detail at the beginning, you may need to be prepared to revise it in the light of what happens as the group is running.

CHAPTER SUMMARY

- Programming is a necessary part of the job of facilitation for most groups.

- It brings with it a number of advantages, perhaps one of the most important being the feeling of security and predictability both for the group and for you. It allows the complexity of group activity to be managed in 'bite-sized chunks'.

- In working out a programme, you will need to take group processes and developmental stages into account and make decisions about what will be the best order in which to make interventions.

- For beginning groupworkers, activities provide some security.

- Activities are only a means to an end. They provide a way of meeting the group's objectives. They have no other purpose and should always have a clear rationale for their use.

- It is very useful to have a toolkit of exercises and activities, either in your mind or on paper, so that you can draw upon them easily. These you will find in books containing games, exercises and activities, and on the shelves of other disciplines – youth work, community work, teaching, child therapy, and so on. You can even steal ideas from television panel games.

Theory

Benson, J (2001) *Working More Creatively with Groups*, 2nd edition. London: Tavistock.

This text contains a short but very useful section on programming and using activities.

Hogan, C (2003) *Practical Facilitation: A toolkit of techniques*. London: Kogan Page.

This is an excellent resource – a comprehensive book with a wealth of ideas and very sound guidance about the facilitation of experiential learning.

Whitaker, DS (1985) *Using Groups to Help People*. London: Routledge and Kegan Paul.

This contains a few pages on activities (pp125–30) in the excellent Part 2, which is unfortunately drastically reduced in the 2nd edition.

Exercises and games

The following is just a small selection of the books of exercises and games that are available. The books by Donna Brandes and colleagues contain a particularly good selection, which are easy to understand and implement. They are intended primarily for children and young people but contain plenty of games that can also be used with adults. The book by Tim Bond is perhaps aimed at an older age group and contains some useful advice on games and their use.

Bond, T (1986) *Games for Social and Life Skills*. Kingston upon Thames: Nelson Thornes.

Brandes, D and Phillip, H (1979) *Gamesters' Handbook No. 1: 140 games for teachers and group leaders.* Kingston upon Thames: Nelson Thornes.

Brandes, D and Phillip, H (1982) *Gamesters' Handbook No. 2.* Kingston upon Thames: Nelson Thornes.

Brandes, D and Norris, J (1998) *Gamesters' Handbook No. 3.* Kingston upon Thames: Nelson Thornes.

Burnard, P (1990) *Learning Human Skills: An experiential guide for nurses.* Oxford: Butterworth-Heinemann.

This text contains specific exercises around John Heron's categories as mentioned in Chapter 3 and is very useful.

Dearling, A and Armstrong, H (1994) *The New Youth Games Book*. Lyme Regis: Russell House Publishing.

Jones, A (1998) *104 Activities that Build: Self-esteem, teamwork, communication, anger management, self discovery, and coping skills.* Richland, WA: Rec Room Publishing.

Lorenz, W (1996) Practical activities for anti-racist work, in Aluffi-Pentini, A and Lorenz, W (eds) *Anti-racist Work with Young People*. Lyme Regis: Russell House Publishing.

Mosley, J and Sonnet, H (2003) *101 Games for Social Skills*. New York: LDA.

Newstrom, JW and Scannell, EE (1996) *Big Book of Business Games: Icebreakers, creativity exercises and meeting energizers.* New York: McGraw-Hill.

Chapter 7
Issues of power and oppression

Introduction

Anti-oppressive practice (AOP) is good groupwork practice, and it is essential to take account of issues of power and oppression at every point in the delivery of a group, from its inception to its completion. We have already mentioned AOP in previous chapters; here, we will summarise the development and changing context for AOP, including that of service-user involvement in all aspects of social work education, and consider some specific issues in more depth.

It can be argued that groupwork has the potential to be less oppressive than other social work methods simply because the numerical balance between workers and service users is in the users' favour. This dynamic can be further enhanced if the balance of power and knowledge in the group can be shared. However, some forms of groupwork where attendance is compulsory can be inherently oppressive, especially where it is difficult for group members to have influence over content or delivery, for example in some groupwork with offenders. Having first discussed some issues of context, we will discuss the importance of considering issues of power and oppression in our planning decisions and in our facilitation of the group.

Context

Your understanding of AOP and your practice, especially groupwork, needs to be viewed in the light of comparatively recent work around the experiences of service users. Understanding AOP is to understand the complexity and history of social work and the relationship between practitioners and service users (Branfield and Beresford, 2006). The context of AOP has developed further since 2003 with the introduction of the current social work degree programme. A change in service-user involvement was at the heart of this development and this has further prompted changes in the discourse and practice:

> Service users and carers [are] to be involved in all aspects of planning, implementing and monitoring of the new degree, including selection processes.
>
> (Burgess, 2004, p5)

AOP is at the core of social work and research, and practice is well developed in this area (Baines, 2007; Dalrymple and Burke, 2006; Dominelli, 2002a, 2002b; Thompson, 2006). The predominant perspective has been for academics with practice experience to write *about* the issues, and to advocate and theorise about the ethics and benefits of AOP. In recent years, there has been a stronger voice from service users who are now publishing their own research, which challenges this paradigm. The argument to develop a more person-centred approach to AOP is gaining momentum, including user-controlled research (UCR) and the reframing and redesigning of service-user involvement from their perspective (Wilson and Beresford, 2000). A definition for 'service user' has been developed by the Shaping Our Lives National User Network (SOL) (2007) and is useful to consider here.

Service user: a definition

Shaping Our Lives National User Network sees 'service user' as an active and positive term, which means more than one thing. It is important that 'service user' should always be based on self-identification. But here are some of the things we think it means.

- *It means that we are in an unequal and oppressive relationship with the State and society.*

- *It is about entitlement to receive welfare services. This includes the past when we might have received them and the present. Some people still need to receive services but are no longer entitled to for many different reasons.*

- *It may mean having to use services for a long time that separate us from other people, and that make people think we are inferior and there is something wrong with us.*

- *Being a service user means that a person can identify and recognise that he or she shares a lot of experiences with a wide range of other people who use services. This might include, for example, young people with experience of being looked after in care, people with learning difficulties, mental health service users, older people, physically and/or sensorily impaired people, people using palliative care services, and people with drug and alcohol problems.*

- *This last point about recognising our shared experiences of using services, whoever we are, makes us powerful and gives us a strong voice to improve the services we are given, and to give us more control and say over what kind of services we want.*

ACTIVITY 7.1

Consider the SOL definition in small groups.

- *What experience of being a service user is there in your group?*

- *If there is experience, does it change, confirm or challenge your view of working with service users? If not, what impact does this have?*

- *How might your knowledge impact on your facilitation?*

COMMENT

The first point in the SOL definition is important and we have to work hard not to perpetuate it. We must not assume a rigid definition of service user or social worker. It is important to check out our own assumptions in this area and to realise that the continuum of 'service user' is complex.

In working in an anti-oppressive way, you need to have a continued willingness to gain support and supervision, to increase your self-awareness, to receive feedback from colleagues and to develop your own understanding of your role in AOP (see Chapters 3 and 5). You are aware that social work often takes place with the most disadvantaged groups in society – those people who are most likely to be excluded from power and influence. With few exceptions, people agree to take part in social work groups not because they require treatment, but because they feel lacking in power. A group's existence may be directly related to the situation that results in them being powerless; SOL confirms this. Some groups are set up specifically to encourage empowerment of individuals or for social action.

Just as we will find the victims of oppression in the membership of the groups, we must also be aware that groups reflect the society from which they are drawn. Group members reflect the same prejudices and discriminatory attitudes that exist in the population as a whole. Some groups may be set up specifically to alter the awareness and behaviour of people who contribute to the disempowerment of others, for example groups for offenders aimed at building victim empathy, or for the perpetrators of domestic violence aimed at understanding the complexities of gender dynamics. As facilitators, we are also carrying our own baggage of oppressive attitudes and belief systems as well as being in a 'powerful' position as organisers of the group.

RESEARCH SUMMARY

The developing roles of service users in social work and in UCR have been documented in three key reports: Beresford (2007), Branfield and Beresford (2006) and Turner and Beresford (2005). These make a strong case for developing the theory and practice of service-user involvement. The rationale is that service users have much to contribute to social work education and they offer a distinct set of discourses to set next to conventional professional and academic social work discussions. Key components of this new practice are that it benefits from being social model-based, inclusive, participative and rights-based. The latter report argues for UCR to be taken more seriously by all key stakeholders of social work research so that there is an increase in the sharing of knowledge about UCR, recognition of its resource implications, and training to support UCR, including in black and minority communities – all to safeguard the future of UCR.

Structuring and planning decisions

Group composition needs careful consideration. In Chapter 5 we suggested that the issues of gender, for example, are relevant in every groupwork context. Groupworkers need to think carefully about the gender implications in all groups, whether for women or for men or for both. Also, taking into consideration the concept of intersectionality, that is, the overlap and interaction of oppressions mentioned in Chapter 5, how do we decide on group composition to maximise the possibilities for AOP? If a group is to be mixed and the unifying factor is not explicitly *around* a social grouping, for example a women's group or a men's group, then we should try to avoid situations where anyone in the group is in a very obvious minority.

Your decisions about the composition of a group will depend upon how well you know your group and the level of trust and understanding you have been able to build up in the preparation and consultation stage, and during the early stages of your group. Lewis and Gutierrez (2003) suggest that we need to begin where group members are and have frank and open discussions as part of the group formation and process, helping the entire group to move consciously through the permutations of the relevant group membership.

Facilitation and co-facilitation

The mix of co-workers and the identity of a single facilitator also need to be considered. Where possible, aim to have a facilitator who can identify and have credibility with all the members of the client group with whom you will be working. If you are working with a group specifically to challenge oppressive or violent behaviour, it can be helpful to 'represent' the victims' perspective in the facilitation of the group. Blacklock (2003, p68) has experience of facilitating programmes for domestic violence perpetrators and he suggests:

> While programmes run by male workers can be challenging, thoughtful and supportive, the emotional effect is nevertheless reduced by not having a female worker. It is akin to the difference between a group of white people discussing their racism and that same discussion being facilitated by black workers.

It is useful to have as wide a range of experience between two facilitators as possible and to build in plenty of preparation time to explore your styles, strengths and weaknesses as well as planning your role(s) in the sessions. If you are building a 'play-list' (Doel, 2006), then allocation of roles within each section can be helpful too. Ensure also that you have access to a mentor or supervisor who provides experience of any perspective you may lack.

Programmes

Any programme needs to be reflective of all the members' cultures and interests. Care needs to be taken so that content, method and style are appropriate. All exercises, games and activities need to be checked to ensure that they do not reflect stereotypical assumptions or cultural bias.

DeLois (2003) reports that her experience of working with lesbian, gay, bisexual and transgender groups has illuminated (for her) the level at which gender is socially constructed, as well as uncovering the depth to which most of us accept assumptions about the meaning of gender. She argues that examining the construction of gender can lead to challenging assumptions and stereotypes about what it means to be male or female. This helps group members to expand their understanding of what it means to be fully human. Brown (1992) suggests putting issues of power and oppression 'on the agenda' or writing them into the ground rules, so that they are a core part of the programme and anyone can raise them at any time. Icebreakers, warm-ups and cool-downs can be used quite specifically to unpack issues of power and oppression. Remember that all games have a power dimension and you can choose to reveal and use the game processes to identify power. Doel (2006, p94) offers activities designed to identify power and oppression:

> *Stereotyping – in pairs, participants deliberately make assumptions about their partner (which newspapers they read, etc.) and share these assumptions.*

> *Power cards – participants take a collection of card descriptions, which apply to them (e.g. woman; white; professional, etc.) and decide how much power (on a scale of one to ten, least to most powerful) they feel each one ascribes them; these can be shared with a partner or the whole group, looking at different situations to see if this changes how they view the power balance.*

It is also important to remember that you will not always have direct control over the programme content, especially if you have a guest participant or speaker, or you invite the group to devise activities themselves. In these situations, you need to be careful to try to ensure that contributions are acceptable and appropriate.

Establishing an anti-oppressive climate based on trust

RESEARCH SUMMARY

Research by Davis and Procter (1989, cited in Brown and Mistry, 1997) suggests that group members import feelings of mistrust, for example women towards men, or black people towards white, due to their experience of oppression from the more powerful groups during their lives.

Groupworkers need to be conscious of this dynamic from the beginning. In other chapters we have talked about preparations, both personal and with colleagues, and about the structure and composition of the group. AOP also depends on your behaviour before, during and after the group, and this is about your skills. Brown and Mistry (1997, pp22–3) refer to some of these skills:

communicating non-verbally and empathetically with individual members – particularly those in minority positions – through the kind of eye contact that conveys recognition, awareness and feeling;

being 'comfortable' in talking about, and the use of language about, race, gender, racism, sexism and other oppressions (e.g. in relation to disability, sexuality, age, class, creed);

relating to a co-worker of a different race or gender in a mutually respectful and equal way . . .;

being prepared to challenge, and not defend, oppressive agency policies and attitudes;

listening to and validating what group members are saying and expressing non-verbally;

being quite open about recognising power issues in the group, including professional power;

being open and ready to acknowledge one's own oppressive or insensitive behaviour when this occurs;

acknowledging the reality of the social conditions prevailing in group members' localities . . .

. . . recognising and responding to the cultural diversity and experience of members.

Ground rules

Ground rules are very important. You model how important they are by how you negotiate them, write them down or present them, and then decide what will happen if individuals 'break' them. Taking time in the first session for exploring, negotiating and deciding the ground rules, and perhaps thinking about how decisions are to be made in the group, are good ways to explore some issues of power. Every group will have 'rules', whether spoken or not, and it can be empowering to raise this issue, and to allow discussion and negotiation. Houston (1990, p29) offers a way of doing this:

> *Making the Rules: When everyone's interest is focussed on rules, suggest that people each write out what they think are the rules operating in your group. In another column they may want to add others that they would like there to be. Displaying the lists and talking them over can give everyone more clarity, and more control of how they run the group. The rules your members invent are likely to be the most creative and appropriate for your group.*

In DeLois (2003) the group wrote their ground rules on a large card and these were read out, one per individual, at the beginning of each session to reaffirm and 'own' them. Another example of 'shaping' or providing a 'rule' was offered by The Members of Women First (2003) to encourage equal participation – the five bean exercise (see page 87). Both examples illustrate power – the first to empower and the second to share power. In your preparation, take time to consider what you want the ground rules to help with in the group and how (Houston, 1990).

Preparing responses to oppressive behaviour

If your preparation and ground rules are well negotiated, you will have done much to create an atmosphere in which the group challenges AOP naturally, as part of the culture. However, you will have to decide how and if you challenge discriminatory remarks or behaviour. It is useful to have practised and prepared the process for a confrontation intervention (see Chapter 5), so you have it up your sleeve. Sometimes, however, if a comment is made in the midst of a busy group, it is quite all right to point out if you are uncomfortable with, or suspect, the tone or intention without having a perfectly formed response. The trick is to remember to comment on the behaviour not the person behind it. Someone may have made a racist or homophobic remark, but it does not make them a bad person. This is a really important distinction. The National Coalition Building Institute (NCBI, 2003) works on the principle that behind every discriminatory remark is some hurt or painful experience that the person may not have explored. Overt remarks and behaviour are sometimes easier to deal with than more subtle forms of oppression, such as a gradual establishment of a dominant group culture, which can be harder to 'see' and deal with – 'That was an interesting point, Anne, perhaps one of the men would like to make it.'

In almost every case you will be better equipped to react appropriately if you have given some thought to situations that might occur and have prepared a couple of possible responses. A discussion with colleagues in advance and afterwards is helpful too.

Worker preparation

We know it is beginning to sound like a broken record, but the bedrock for good practice comes from developing, and continuing to develop, self-awareness and consciousness around how you feel about your gender, your race, your class, your sexuality, your religion, your age, your physical ability and your mental health. You need to make a conscious effort to look at your own 'stuff' and how your relationship with these issues will impact on your ability to facilitate processes around them. Revisiting the Johari exercise in Chapter 3 will reinforce this (see page 50). This work may be particularly challenging for people who 'choose' to keep their identities private or hidden, especially lesbians, gays, bisexual and transgendered men and women, and people who have a medical or physical condition that is not self-evident. These groups are particularly susceptible to internal oppression, that is, internalising and rejecting the stereotype of their 'tribe' because it is too painful or scary to own it, and, in defence, persecuting 'their' tribe. It is never acceptable to 'out' or reveal a private identity; it is *always* the responsibility of the person concerned. It is good practice to create a climate that actively accepts and includes 'hidden' identities by using inclusive behaviour and language.

Identifying oppressive or discriminatory behaviour or language

In understanding and learning to identify oppressive or discriminatory behaviour or language, it becomes even more important that we develop our self-awareness within all of our zones (see Chapter 3), and acknowledge and understand the impact of our own gender, identity, communication styles, personality and learning preferences. Remember that we are likely to find it hard to 'see' or 'feel' discrimination or oppressive issues if we have grown up within the dominant culture or discourse and have never challenged our own assumptions. In its Prejudice Reduction Trainers Workshop, the NCBI offers two exercises called 'Identity groups' and 'First thoughts', which we find useful here.

- **Identity groups** – Participants are invited to form groups or 'tribes' that they feel they identify with or belong to, for example black working women, white middle-class men, people living alone, people who are stepchildren and single mothers with children. Each group is invited to identify unhelpful stereotyping of their group and to write down 'What stereotyping statements do you dislike and never again want people to say, think or do about your group?' They then present their reports to the rest of the workshop. A facilitated discussion of the exercise follows.

- **First thoughts** – This is a pairs exercise for people from different identity groups. Each invites and encourages his or her partner to 'make mistakes about my group or tribe' as an opportunity to explore in safety the first discriminatory thoughts that they might have about each other's tribe. Partners take it in turns and then discuss the experience. Some of these 'thoughts' may well have been articulated in the group reports.

We have found the most important aspects of these exercises are to recognise that we all belong to 'tribes' and 'groups', and that we all make assumptions and project our prejudicial thoughts on to them. It might be useful to explore these exercises with your colleagues.

These exercises are challenging and must be facilitated with care, allowing plenty of time for discussion and consideration of the issues raised.

Mullender (2003, p207) provides excellent advice:

> *As long as we think in terms of multiple strengths that present in overlapping and interacting diversities within any group, and not in essentialist dichotomized categories, and provided we do not ground our approach in an assumption that there are universal answers to human problems, then there is no reason why coming together in groups should not make men more able to rethink their social positioning and women to feel stronger.*

CHAPTER SUMMARY

- Anti-oppressive practice is at the core of good groupwork practice.

- Power and oppression are both personal and pervasive.

- The influence of service users in all aspects of social work education and practice is, rightly, changing and increasing.

- Attention to anti-oppressive practice is vital in all aspects of group facilitation, specifically in relation to planning, structuring and programming, especially with clearly negotiated ground rules.

- You need to prepare yourself so that you can be effective in identifying and confronting oppressive language and behaviour.

- You need to be self-aware and understand the impact of your identity on the service users and the context of the group programme.

FURTHER READING

Beresford, P (2007) *The Changing Roles and Tasks of Social Work from Service Users' Perspectives: A literature informed discussion paper.* Shaping Our Lives National User Network. Available online at www.gscc.org.uk.

This paper discusses the changing context for service-user involvement in social work and provides a literature review of articles on social work that provide a service-user perspective.

Cohen, M and Mullender, A (eds) (2003) *Gender and Groupwork.* London and New York: Routledge.

This is a collection of contributions that in total summarises the history of gender-based groups for both women and men, and outlines a wide range of examples of groups in different contexts.

Doel, M (2006) *Using Groupwork.* London: Routledge.

This contains an excellent mix of practice examples placed in the context of AOP.

Doel, M and Sawdon, C (1999) *The Essential Groupworker.* London: Jessica Kingsley.

This has a very useful chapter on power and oppression in groupwork.

Mistry, T and Brown, A (eds) (1997) *Race and Groupwork.* London: Whiting and Birch.

This book brings together a selection of material involving the issues facing black groupworkers and the groupwork needs of service users from minority communities.

Chapter 8
Coping with unexpected or unhelpful responses

Introduction

The title of this chapter provided us with some head-scratching. We wanted to avoid titles like 'Dealing with problems' because, as we will see, some of the situations we want to cover are not problems at all, but just things that happen that we do not expect, or for which we have not planned. These can be tricky situations, things we find difficult or challenging, or events or actions outside the group that make our job more difficult, as well as people taking on problematic or unhelpful roles in the group (which can include ourselves or our co-workers!). So, a note on terminology: we will try to avoid terms that pathologise individuals, but some situations are difficult and problematic so we will use a number of different terms – issues, difficulties, situations, and so on. What they have in common is that they cause us some discomfort as facilitators and are things we need to think about and work on.

RESEARCH SUMMARY

Williams (1966) identified a number of common anxieties among trainee group facilitators. These were:

- *encountering unmanageable resistance;*

- *losing control of the group;*

- *excessive hostility breaking out;*

- *acting out by group members;*

- *overwhelming dependency demands;*

- *group disintegration.*

Williams' research is interesting in a number of ways, not least in that it highlights how little imagination trainees have in thinking about what might go wrong. Whitaker (2001) states, I have a **sizeable** *list of such descriptions. The situations referred to include: . . . (p143; our emphasis), and then goes on to list 30 different difficult scenarios.*

Informal feedback that we have taken from students about their groupwork facilitation indicates that the area in which they feel least comfortable is dealing with the difficulties that occur. By their nature, these situations are difficult to plan for. It would be equally as impossible to be prepared in advance for the vast range of events that can happen in groupwork as it would be in working with individuals. Nevertheless, dealing with problems in groups, where you are working with a number of service users rather than just one, and where you may be exposing your practice to colleagues, can be a lot more frightening. These are understandable fears. Our hope in this chapter is that we can help to eradicate or reduce some of these fears – that we can prepare you for some of the situations that you may perceive as problems. You should be able to avoid or alleviate some situations by good planning and by thinking out in advance what you would do if your fears were realised. Additionally, we hope that we can provide some reassurance.

Thinking about problem areas and responses

When things go wrong, there can be a tendency to see the difficulty as lying with the group members. Frequently, however, 'unhelpful' or 'difficult' behaviour by individuals or the group as a whole is more usefully understood as a symptom of some other problem related to the group process, the planning or resources of the group, or the conduct of the group-worker(s).

Douglas (1991) identifies five potentially problematic areas for group facilitators.

• **How the facilitator(s) perform the role** – what they know and how well they know it, their style of facilitation, their level of skill and the roles they adopt in the group, their aims and objectives, and the extent to which all of these are congruent with those of any other facilitators involved.

• **Supervision, training and development of groupworkers** – this area is closely related to the first.

• **Group members** – their individual characteristics and behaviour.

• **The group as a unit or system (whole-group problems)** – problems that arise out of the way the group is structured and those that are to do with the nature and quality of the group's performance and processes.

• **The conditions under which the group operates** – external factors such as how it is organised, the venue and time, the resources allocated to it, and issues to do with colleagues, managers and the community; internal factors such as the numbers, the construction of the group and how it is designed.

Learning to deal with problematic roles or whole-group issues is often a matter of experience. It is impossible to give advice on how to deal with every conceivable groupwork problem. It is better to give you some general responses that you may apply in a variety of situations. However, for more detailed discussion of specific difficult situations, see Douglas (1991) and Whitaker (2001).

Difficulties arising from the group itself and its members

Reconceptualising 'problems'
When faced with a difficult or unexpected situation in the group itself, we need to be able to analyse what is going on, so that we can make an appropriate response.

• **Problem or opportunity?** – It is useful, as Whitaker (2001) suggests, to understand what is happening as an opportunity, rather than a problem. If a group member launches a verbal attack on another, for example, it may be an opportunity to have a useful discussion about issues such as the relationships in the group as a whole, acceptable ways of confronting, or the group rules, or to provide feedback. Everything that happens in a group has a cause; sometimes the cause lies outside the group, sometimes within it. In either case, difficult situations indicate to us that something requires our attention. See them as warnings or as symptoms. Try to work out the cause and then you may be able to find the cure.

• **Problem for whom?** – What may be seen as a big problem by the groupworker may not necessarily be a problem for anyone else. A useful question to ask yourself is 'For whom is this a problem?' If the only answer is the facilitator, then you know it is something that you are going to have to think about in terms of yourself and either adjust to or live with.

If the answer is an individual in the group, you need to decide what action to take to protect that person from harm. If it is a whole-group problem, you will need to think in terms of a whole-group response. If it is a problem for people outside the group, you will probably need to do some work with neighbours, colleagues or whoever it concerns.

CASE STUDY

A group was running very successfully and had reached a stage where a high level of trust and cooperation existed; people had become open and ready to help each other. The facilitators were very pleased and, for the next session, planned an activity that they felt would be good in taking this work forward. When the session got under way, none of the group members would take the activity seriously. There was much joking, larking around and contagious laughing. The facilitators felt that the session had been a waste of time and felt quite angry with the group for being so flippant.

Here we have a situation that seems to be a problem only for the facilitators. The group is going well and people are enjoying themselves at the same time as deriving considerable benefit. Perhaps they are avoiding something, but it is just as likely that they are doing more work on building group cohesion or even just having a well-earned rest before returning to work.

- **Who benefits?** – Many situations that you perceive as problems are actually functional in some way, either for the group as a whole or for individuals. You will remember from Chapter 5 that we discussed the processes that occur in groups. You need to think of these difficult situations in terms of group process.

CASE STUDY

Social workers in a fostering and adoption team are facilitating a group for people who have applied to be adoptive parents. In every session, Winston monopolises the situation by continuously talking, interrupting others and never letting anyone else speak. This situation may be functional for both Winston and the rest of the group. Maybe it allows them to avoid something they find uncomfortable, perhaps feelings of sadness about infertility, anxiety about the approval process or fear about looking after children. Whitaker (2001) sees this sort of situation as arising out of focal group conflict – that is, a solution to some underlying conflict, perhaps between addressing some of these feelings and avoiding them (see Chapter 5).

- **Is this the end of the world?** – Although anxieties may run high, it is unlikely that anything disastrous is going to happen. No one is likely to die or even be badly hurt and you will not lose your job or your practice opportunity unless you have been very negligent (no guarantees, of course!). Furthermore, most situations can be recovered. When we make a mistake, we nearly always get another chance to do it again and get it right next time. Problems do have a habit of recurring if not resolved, so you will probably get another chance. We all make mistakes and there is no reason why you cannot return to a difficult issue deliberately during the next session . . . after you have had a chance to think it through. Remember: you learn more from your mistakes than from what you do well.

Responding to individual and whole-group situations

Brown (1992) provides a useful framework of possible responses to difficult situations that may arise out of individual and whole-group scenarios.

- **Do 'nothing'** – It is a good idea to wait a little while before making any intervention, provided no one is being hurt. Let the mud settle. Learn to wait, watch and listen (see Chapter 3, page 52 on listening and questioning). This way you are more likely to attend to the needs of the group rather than your own. It is easy to panic and do something that will make you feel more comfortable rather than think about the group. It is important to give yourself a little time, first to make sure you understand what is happening, second to see if the problem will resolve itself or turn out not to be a problem, and third to allow the group members themselves to deal with it. People who can tolerate silence, for example, tend to make better groupworkers. The solutions that members come up with are likely to be much more powerful and enduring than those of the facilitators, and allowing them to do so is strengthening and empowering. Of course, if the problem persists, it is the responsibility of the facilitator to intervene.

- **Indirect approaches** – The worker does not confront the situation directly, or indeed even mention that there is a difficulty, but finds an indirect way of dealing with the problem. For example, the simple tactic of sitting next to someone can be very effective in providing non-verbal support without drawing unwanted attention to the individual, or can make it easier to control undesirable behaviour. In Chapter 6, we discussed how you could use the group programme to deal with situations that arise.

CASE STUDY

In a group for young people, one member had great difficulty in finding personal control. Typical behaviour was to be inappropriate, noisy and unintentionally very disruptive, so that it was hard to make any progress. In the light of prior knowledge of the member's home circumstances, and after much discussion, the facilitators concluded that the behaviour arose because of the member's difficulty in trusting anyone in the group. In the following session, they introduced an exercise where the group took turns leading blindfolded members around the building. Here the programme was adapted to include an exercise to help the young person to start building trust in the others.

- **Direct approaches** – Direct approaches involve making explicit reference to the problem. Brown (1992) gives three categories of direct approaches.

  - *Speak directly to the individual at the centre of the problem* – For example, where the group is treating an individual as a scapegoat, a solution might be to say to the person that he or she always seems to be getting the blame for things that go wrong in the group. Where someone is monopolising the conversation in the group, you can point out to the person that she or he is doing all the work in the group, and it is time to have a rest and let the others have a turn.

- *Speak directly to the rest of the group* – 'I am wondering why you all seem to blame Mary, when something goes wrong here' or 'You seem to be allowing Brian to do all the talking tonight'; sometimes saying 'What is . . . ', naming the issue, is a sufficient strategy to resolve a difficulty.

- *Speak to the group as a whole* – 'I am thinking that we don't seem to be very together tonight. There seems to be a lot of tension around. Has anyone else noticed that? What do you think is going on just now? Maybe we can talk about this for a while and see if we can find a better way forward.'

Of these three direct strategies, Brown suggests that the last is to be preferred, as it does not reinforce possible splits in the group, nor does it locate the difficulty in a particular person or persons.

- **Make contact outside the group** – Before deciding to make contact with a member outside the group, you will need to consider the following questions: In seeing this person alone, am I missing an opportunity to facilitate a problem that lies in the group but is manifesting itself through this individual? Even if I am satisfied that this is a difficulty concerning this individual, would it be beneficial to try to resolve it in the group, so that all the members can benefit from the intervention? In seeing this person outside the group, am I perhaps making things worse for the person by pathologising him or her, or worse for the group by entering into a special relationship with this one individual? We suggest that making contact outside the group is really a last-choice strategy.

Difficulties arising from external factors

There are a large number of difficulties that may arise that have nothing to do with the individual members, the whole group or the quality of the group facilitation. Groups do not operate in vacuums and things that happen outside affect them. These can be to do with colleagues or the agency (see Chapter 4). Funding can disappear; venues become unavailable; there can be problems with the local community, neighbours, the press, and so on. In our work with quite experienced groupworkers we have found, time and time again, that they find these external problems the most frustrating and at times hardest to resolve, perhaps because many of them arise from factors beyond their control. Here, again, we cannot provide solutions to every scenario, but you may find the following ideas interesting and useful.

Force-field analysis

When facing a difficulty, especially a complex difficulty, it can be very useful to break the situation down into its component parts. *Force-field analysis* is a simple but powerful system of analysing problem situations. It was devised by the psychologist Kurt Lewin, 'the father of group dynamics'. Lewin (1951) took the concept from topology and applied it to human situations. At the heart of the concept is the idea that we can regard any problem situation as being held in a balance or *equilibrium* due to competing forces acting upon it (see Figure 8.1).

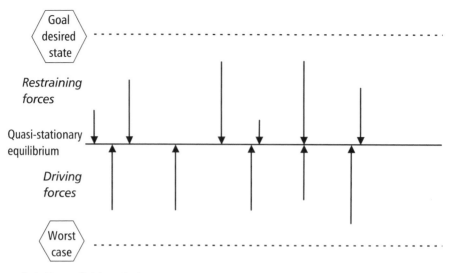

Figure 8.1: Force-field analysis

In this model one set of forces, the *driving forces*, are conceptualised as pushing the situation towards the state we desire, the *goal*, while another set, the *restraining forces*, are pushing in the opposite direction, away from the desired state towards an even worse scenario. Lewin argued that it must be the case that the situation was in equilibrium; otherwise, things would either improve or worsen dramatically. To reflect the fact that the situation is not held in a completely stationary equilibrium, he used the expression *quasi-stationary equilibrium* to refer to the current state.

Figure 8.1 is a very basic depiction of the model. However, we can construct a more sophisticated diagram using larger and smaller arrows to show strong and weak forces, and we can show forces that are in direct opposition to each other. Figure 8.2 gives an example

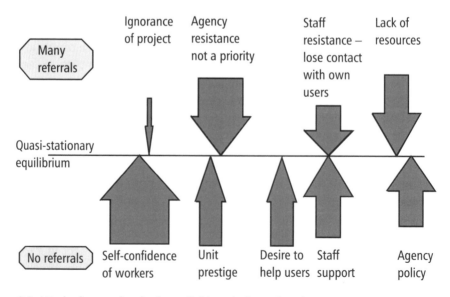

Figure 8.2: Worked example of a force-field analysis – referrals

of a force-field analysis of a situation where a group is not getting enough referrals. Note how staff support and resistance directly oppose each other.

ACTIVITY *8.1*

Identify a problem you are currently facing, or something you would like to change in your life. It could be a personal problem, such as deciding that you would like to lose weight, or a professional problem, such as deciding you want to work less hard. Use force-field analysis to work out the forces that are preventing you from getting to where you want to be and those that are helping you.

COMMENT

Force-field analysis can help you with situations other than groupwork problems. It can help you to weigh up the pros and cons in a number of areas. It is also useful in risk analysis to identify hazards and strengths (Brearley, 1982; Kelly, 1996).

Having analysed the factors in a problematic situation, you should be able to make some decisions about what action might be appropriate. In our example in Figure 8.2, we could decide to try to increase staff support or work to further increase the self-confidence of the staff. Alternatively, we could increase people's knowledge of the project and thereby remove the 'Ignorance' arrow, or we could reassure people that they will not lose contact with their service users. However, Lewin argued that it was better to remove or weaken restraining forces than to increase the driving forces. His reason for this, from topology, was that the more forces that are present in a situation, the greater is the tension and therefore the more difficult it is to move the equilibrium.

Mentoring

Facilitating a group either on your own or with a co-worker is a difficult and demanding task. Groupwork is almost by definition more complex than one-to-one work, as there are so many more variables and you are engaged with so many more people and limitless situations that are beyond the scope of individual therapy (Riva, 2013). Facilitators come under pressure from the group. The feelings aroused in the group and the workers can be very powerful. Being aware and coping with your own feelings, and recognising and responding to emotion in the group, while conducting the group programme and following through the group aims all at once is far from easy. Having one or more co-facilitators is often a great help, for the reasons given earlier, but the co-working relationship itself introduces another variable in the group equation. It is very difficult for co-facilitators to sort out difficulties in their relationship on their own. Often they will conspire together *not* to discuss them.

For all these reasons it is important for groupworkers to have someone – a mentor – with whom they can discuss what is happening in the group (and the co-worker relationship if there is one) and to help them think of ways of sorting out issues. During mentoring sessions, the workers can explore the power relationships between them. Issues such as sectarianism, sexuality, race and gender need to be addressed by co-workers in terms of how they work together, what role models they provide, and how they deal with conscious or unconscious sectarianism, racism or sexism directed towards one or more of them. A mentor is a very useful resource. We think that for the new groupworker it is essential.

Students on placement are fortunate to have built-in supervision in the form of the practice teacher. However, research (Lindsay, 2005; Scally and Lindsay, 1997) shows that the practice teacher may not have much groupwork expertise. In these circumstances, before embarking on a groupwork project, students should negotiate with their practice teachers to ensure that they have access to regular mentoring from someone who has the necessary experience and knowledge.

Mentoring is not the same as supervision. Supervision usually occurs between the worker and the person who has responsibility for agency accountability for the quality of his or her work – for example, the line manager or the practice teacher. Mentoring is about providing a forum for the open exploration of the issues arising in the group. The same person can conduct the two, but there may be situations where it is inappropriate for the practice teacher or line manager to undertake this role. We have discussed above the situation where the supervisor does not have enough experience in this area of work. Alternatively, it may be that there are issues to do with the formal or informal power relationships between the co-workers and the supervisor; there may be issues of seniority or inter-agency relationships; the balance in terms of gender or ethnicity may be inappropriate for the group in mind.

Mentoring in general, and groupwork mentoring in particular, are important subjects in their own right and we have space only to indicate a few basic points.

- Choose the mentor carefully to ensure a productive working relationship.

- Draw up a mentoring agreement or contract.

- Arrange for mentoring to start from the group planning stage.

- Plan in and diary mentoring sessions, just like the other groupwork sessions, to ensure they happen and do not collude to avoid them when things are rocky.

- Make sure that all understand the focus and agenda of mentoring sessions.

- The mentor should adopt a pro-active approach in mentoring sessions.

- Everyone involved is equally responsible for the success of the mentoring arrangement.

DeLucia-Waack (2002, cited in DeLucia-Waack and Nitza, 2013) suggests the following agenda for mentoring sessions.

- **Reporting** what has happened in the most recent session.

- **Reflection** on what has happened – what worked and what didn't and especially why, what felt good and what felt bad and why, and how the facilitators worked together.

- **Integration** of what has happened in terms of theoretical understanding and group aims.

- **Planning** of what happens next: to what extent the programme needs to be adjusted; activities that need to be added or taken out; and the way in which process issues need to be addressed.

- **Evaluation** of the mentoring session – that which was helpful or unhelpful, that which was learnt, and that which should happen in the next mentoring session.

Before we leave this chapter, we would like to refer you to some rules for survival suggested by Benson (2001).

- **Do not become over-involved or self-sacrificing** – Allow people to struggle. You are not a miracle worker. You cannot hope to rescue and save people all the time and solve all their problems for them. Sometimes you just have to sit by and watch them suffer as they work it out for themselves. You cannot take responsibility away from them.

- **Do not push the river upstream** – From physics, Boyle's law states that *to every action there is an equal and opposite reaction*. Sometimes the more you push a group, the more it resists. The more you talk, the less the group members listen. The more you do, the less they do. The more you try to help, the more they stick to unhelpful ways. Give yourself a break. Go with the flow. Work with the group where it is.

- **Do not beat yourself up** – Learn to forgive yourself. You will make mistakes. We all do. Think of yourself as someone who is learning a very hard job. Remember that we learn both from our mistakes and from what we do well.

- **Cultivate goodwill** – First, keep in mind the positive reasons for having the group in the first place. Second, remember that the members would not be attending if they were not getting something of value from the experience. So when they want to criticise, shock, please or manipulate you, do not fight back. Just accept it as an opportunity to help them understand what they are doing. From this, they can find ways that are more positive for themselves.

- **Make up your own rules** – Remember that most of what is written about groupwork is done from experience. Rely on your own experience also. The rules do not cover every eventuality and sometimes your gut feelings will be more important than rules. Be creative. Improvise. Try out things for yourself. If they work, that is good – you will know to use them again. If they do not, that is good too – you have learnt something new.

Here is another rule, this time from us.

- **Get your feet wet** – There is no better way of learning about groupwork than doing it. So long as you have planned it well and made sure you are well supported, it will be fine. Have a go. It is extremely unlikely that you will hurt anyone – especially yourself. The chances are people will find your work very helpful and you will be very satisfied with your efforts. There comes a time when you certainly are not going to get any further by sitting there reading this book.

CHAPTER SUMMARY

- Facilitating groups can be worrying. Groupwork involves working with a high degree of complexity and unpredictability. Things rarely go exactly to plan and you will need to be prepared to deal with some unexpected situations.

- It is useful to realise that this is a normal part of groupwork facilitation and not a disaster.

- Good planning is at the foundation of groupwork practice and will carry you through a long way. Nevertheless, you need to prepare yourself for the unexpected. One way is to realise what is likely to go wrong. Another is to be able to analyse what is happening.

- Difficulties can manifest themselves in a number of different ways and there is a variety of ways in which you can conceptualise these situations and respond. You will also need to have a repertoire of responses that you can apply to most situations.

- Having someone who is not directly involved in the group can be a great help in untangling issues, in relation to what is happening either in the group, or between the facilitators or between the group and the outside.

FURTHER READING

Brown, A (1992) *Groupwork*, 3rd edition. Aldershot: Ashgate Publishing.

Brown identifies 'difficult' behaviours and provides a number of possible responses, categorised as described above.

Doel, M and Sawdon, C (1999) *The Essential Groupworker.* London: Jessica Kingsley.

In this you will find descriptions and analysis of eight behaviours that groupworkers can find challenging.

Douglas, T (1991) *A Handbook of Common Groupwork Problems.* London: Tavistock/Routledge.

This text is entirely devoted to identifying and resolving difficult issues that may arise in groups.

Whitaker, DS (2001) *Using Groups to Help People*, 2nd edition. Hove: Brunner-Routledge.

This has a useful chapter entitled 'Problems and opportunities', in which the author identifies and categorises group situations that you may consider problematic. The author analyses these and provides helpful and straightforward advice on how to deal with them.

Chapter 9
Monitoring, recording and evaluating your work

Introduction

This chapter considers the tasks needed to gather evidence about your groupwork projects, in order to demonstrate success to different audiences and stakeholders, to enable you to learn and develop your practice and to disseminate your findings. As in all other chapters, we advocate developing a systematic approach to monitoring, recording and evaluating your groupwork from personal and interpersonal perspectives, as well as throughout all aspects of development, that is, before, during and after your project. We will refer back to ideas introduced in Chapters 2 and 3, including reflective practices and the 'Model for planning' pro forma (see Figure 2.1, page 25), where we suggested writing down the *directional phases* and introduced the notion of SMART criteria for your project.

Recording

However much it is stressed that recording what goes on in a group is a tool of personal development as well as a means of recording the group's life, it is a ploy regarded with great antipathy by even professional groupworkers.

(Douglas, 1995, p155)

It is not too strong to say that many people find record-keeping the least attractive of all the tasks that a groupworker undertakes. Considering that Prince (1996) estimates that record-keeping takes up approximately a fifth of a social worker's time (and we suggest that this is an estimation that holds true for groupwork as well as other social work activities), the task can be irksome indeed. However, for good practice, and the requirements for many social work degrees, it is not optional. Much has been written about recording for social work generally. The skills needed are common to most social work interventions. You will be aware of a number of excellent texts that cover this (Coulshed and Orme, 2006; Dutton and Kohli, 1996; Prince, 1996; Trevithick, 2005b). Here, we restrict ourselves to a discussion of recording as it applies to groupwork. We start with a brief summary of the reasons for keeping a record of your group.

- Reporting to colleagues and management after the group has ended, to inform and convince of the value of groupwork.

- Providing information for yourself and your colleagues who are supervising service users about each individual's participation, the perceived impact of the group on him or her, and the fulfilment of statutory obligations (e.g. attendance).

- Providing feedback to group members, to develop further plans for the group.

- Keeping a record for yourself about group progress, in order to develop your skills, and to improve potential benefits of the group.

- Providing information for the post-group review.

- Providing training materials for colleagues and students.

- Providing information for more formal research and evaluation.

- Providing evidence of competence as a student social worker.

We are aware that you may need to produce records of your work with groups in order to satisfy the demands of your course or accrediting body. Consequently, we later provide a format (see Figure 9.1, pages 132–3) to enable you to do this.

Recording groups

ACTIVITY 9.1

Watch a 'soap' on television and make a written record of about 15 minutes of it. Try to capture the process as well as the content of what happens. Pay attention to the underlying emotions, to what is not said, and to what is said but differs from what is meant and what is the actual case.

COMMENT

Did you find that difficult? Some of the difficulties that you may have encountered are probably similar to the problems we have when we record groups. We now consider what these may be.

- *Recording groupwork is complicated. You will remember that we discussed in Chapter 3 the need to monitor what is occurring in a group at four different levels: the personal (regarding your own feelings and thoughts), the individual, the interpersonal and the whole group. This, of course, also applies to recording the group. Furthermore, in Chapter 5 we discussed content and process, and how the concept of process has greater significance in groupwork because of the multiple relationships that exist. It follows, then, that we need to give sufficient attention to the recording of process as well as content.*

- *Since recording groups is more complicated and there is more to capture, we may find that the traditional methods of recording that we use elsewhere are not adequate and we need to find more creative approaches.*

- *When we are in a co-working relationship, we need to have an accurate shared and agreed perception of what has happened in the group.*

- *If you are working with people who have been referred to your group by another worker, you need to provide some information for them. It can be somewhat unnerving to have your work coming under the scrutiny of your colleagues.*

- *Groupwork often has to justify itself in a way that individual work does not (we often wonder why this should be). Consequently, we may have a greater need to record what took place so as to be able to produce evidence of effectiveness.*

Methods of recording

Written

For some purposes (e.g. reporting to an agency), it will be sufficient to record a brief summary of events of each session, including attendance, topics covered, notable events and notes about the way individuals participated and responded. You can incorporate these notes into a final report, or they can form the basis of notes in official case records.

You may decide that you need a more detailed record for the purposes of facilitation (e.g. changes in patterns of behaviour, points of tension, issues and themes, challenges to groupworkers, prevailing moods), or to provide evidence of your groupwork competence. To assist with this we provide a pro forma in Figure 9.1.

STUDENT NAME: Co-worker/s:

Group title:

Date: Session number:

Attendance:
    Present:

    Absent (Comment):

Where we all sat:

Use lines to indicate:
Affinities ....
Conflicts - - - - - - -

Aim of this session:

Plan for this session:

Facilitation roles – who had responsibility for what:

Group process
Stage of group development:

Processes this session:
    Atmosphere/mood:

    Themes/patterns:

Figure 9.1 Groupwork record

What happened (group values and norms; helpful roles and unhelpful roles; communication between members; attraction/conflict):

What I did during the session:

Evaluation

What went well and why:

What I/we could have improved upon and why:

Facilitation issues:

    Planning :

    Maintaining :

    Monitoring :

    Intervening :

Co-working issues:
What went well — support, modelling, sharing tasks, etc.

What could have been improved upon – preparation, competitiveness, communication, splitting by group, etc.

What I learnt from this piece of work :

What my future learning needs are :

Figure 9.1 Groupwork record (continued)

Video and sound recording

To improve your level of skill, or to consider group process in some depth, it may be appropriate to consider video or sound recording at least one session or parts of several sessions, selecting one or two passages for close analysis and reflection. If you are intending to use video, you will need to discuss it with colleagues, co-facilitators and the group, and consider some ground rules and an opt-out as necessary. The knowledge that they are being filmed can make some people very nervous, so you will need to run some familiarisation exercises so that they can become comfortable with the medium – just getting them to tell a story or joke on camera may be enough. People can be very interested in seeing themselves on screen and you will probably need to arrange for them to view the recording. A video record is also a good way for your practice teacher to observe your practice without actually being present, which in some groups would be intrusive and inappropriate. Issues of confidentiality and use of material must be considered with care, as it would not be helpful or appropriate for your groupwork project to star on an internet broadcast site such as youtube.com.

Members' records

Group members may value having a record of the group. It is easy to forget what has been achieved; a group record is a useful way of making sure that the group and individuals do not lose sight of that. It may be appropriate for the group members to construct the record themselves, either as a written record, or perhaps using artwork, photography or music. With written records, the group may be helped by exercises such as sentence completion, for example: 'The best thing about tonight was . . .' or 'The person who made the biggest contribution today was . . .'. Remember that some group members may have problems with writing, so it may be best if one of the workers acts as scribe.

Evaluation

Evaluation is at the core of evidence-based practice and is a key skill for social workers. All of this is in the spirit of 'growing groupwork'. Doel (2006) offers a helpful chapter on this and advocates the need for the development of expertise in gathering evidence and for evaluation so that the value of groupwork is more widely known and available to practitioners:

> If groupwork is making a difference, we need reliable and detailed information about this 'difference' in order to build a case for sustained groupwork service.
>
> *(Doel, 2006, p157)*

What are you evaluating?

Preston-Shoot (2007, p181) suggests that evaluation may focus on the following.

• *Reactions of the groupworkers and members.*

• *Changes in attitudes.*

• *Acquisition of knowledge and skills.*

• *Behavioural change.*

- *Organisational change.*

- *Benefits to members and their carers or those for whom they care.*

You will be evaluating a number of things for different purposes. Kirkpatrick (cited in Hogan, 2003, p423) offers a model for evaluation. First introduced in 1959, this has stood the test of time. We offer it here as a framework with our own additions.

Reactions or short-term evaluation

These are the types of activities that give you information about how participants and you and your co-facilitators are feeling about the programme. In here we would add the concept of *formative evaluation* – evaluating as you go along so that you can adjust and adapt the programme as needed. The methods you might use are many, from informal chats during breaks, questionnaires, or a check-in at the start of the group, to a written or online form at the end of the programme. Below is an example of formative and participative evaluation that we have found helpful. It is an extension of the sentence completion exercise.

At the end of a session give out a blank card to all participants and facilitators, and invite them to write a sentence starting with, for example: 'I have . . . ', 'I know . . . ', 'I will . . . ', 'I learnt today that . . . ' or 'I feel . . . ', 'Next session I need . . . '. You can use different prompts to gauge different responses. Collect all the cards in and read them yourself; this will give you a flavour of the group. At the start of the next session give out the cards, ensuring that people do not get their own cards, and go round the group reading the cards. Remember to explain the task, its purpose and the whole process to the members before you begin, to allow everyone to understand how it works.

Learning and behaviour

It is unlikely that you will be attempting to 'test' or 'assess' participants in a formal educational context. However, inviting participants to record, monitor and understand how their learning and behaviour have changed during the course of the groupwork project can be very empowering for service users, and for you and your co-facilitators. We favour methods that are either cooperative between facilitator and participants or autonomous, including journal writing and self- and peer-assessment. Asking the same questions at the beginning, mid-point and end of a group will offer a story or progression. Table 9.1 is an example of a simple formative evaluation form.

Results

Agencies and organisations usually want to find out if the time, energy and resources invested in a groupwork project have been worth it. This is the direct link to the *directional phases* we invited you to record in the planning (see Figure 2.1, page 25) and to the SMART objectives, particularly M – measurable (see page 28). Evaluation will be so much easier if you have taken time at the beginning, middle and end of your project to look at, discuss with participants if appropriate, articulate and record in detail what success looks like.

Evaluation for practice evidence

So far, we have discussed evaluation in terms of how successful the group has been in meeting its objectives. However, you may be required by your degree programme to

Evaluation and Feedback Form	Group:	Date:
1. What were the most useful things for you today?		
2. What were the least useful things for you today?		
3. If you found it difficult to participate in the group today, can you say why and offer reasons and suggestions on how the session could be improved?		
4. Next session I want more . . .		
5. Next session I want less . . .		
6. Do you have any feedback or suggestions about the facilitation or co-facilitation?		
Please add any other comments that you would like to make.		
Thank you	Name (optional):	

Table 9.1: A simple formative evaluation form

evaluate your own practice in order to provide evidence of your competence. When we evaluate anything, we need to be able to make a comparison between how things were and how they are now. In this way, we can tell if anything has changed (for the better or for the worse). This holds equally for your evaluation of your practice. You need to know the skills, knowledge and values you brought to the piece of work, and the added skills and knowledge you have now that you have completed the work. This should allow you to reflect on the process of your learning: What happened that brought about that change in me?

Preston-Shoot (2007, p185) provides a useful *personal audit* that will help you to establish for yourself your level of practice at the outset of the group.

- *What skills and knowledge do you bring to your practice?*
- *What are your strengths in groupwork and social (care) practice?*
- *What roles and styles come easily to you?*
- *What do you hope to contribute to this group?*
- *In what areas do you wish to improve or develop your practice?*
- *What are you hoping to learn from working with others in this group?*

In Chapter 5 we discussed 'tuning in' in preparation for the first session and, of course, this preparatory work is essential before every session. It will also provide you with the personal audit and will provide important evidence of your competence to practise. Practice teachers and supervisors often ask for this and so we provide a possible pro forma in Table 9.2.

Pro forma for tuning in to a groupwork session

Session: Number . . . of . . . (e.g. Session Number 3 of 8)

1. What are the main issues that have presented themselves in the group so far?

2. What are the issues now in terms of:

   - the whole group?
     - (a) What stage is the group at in terms of group development (e.g. forming, storming, etc.; and inclusion, control, affection, separation)?
     - (b) How cohesive is the group?
     - (c) What issues of control and power are evident?
     - (d) What is the prevailing mood and atmosphere?
     - (e) Other issues.

   - the individual?
     - (a) Are there any individuals who seem isolated? uncomfortable? unhappy?
     - (b) Are individuals adopting particular roles that are either helpful or unhelpful to the group?
     - (c) Are you aware of anything in their personal lives that might have a bearing on how the individuals are in the group?

   - the interpersonal?
     - (a) What pairings or subgroups are evident? How are these impacting on the group?
     - (b) What issues are evident in terms of attraction and conflict?

   - the personal (including interpersonal between co-facilitators)?
     - (a) What are my feelings about facilitating the group?
     - (b) What are my feelings about groupings or individuals in the group?
     - (c) What is the character of my relationship with my co-faciliator?
       - (i) Are there unresolved issues between my co-facilitator and me?
       - (ii) How might these have a bearing on how we work together?

3. Is there any unfinished business from the previous session to which I need to attend in this session?

4. What is the aim of this session?

5. What is the plan or programme for the session?

6. Facilitation roles: Who has responsibility for what?

7. What knowledge do I need for this session?

8. What skills might be most relevant? What is my degree of confidence and competence in using these?

9. Values: What are the issues around oppression, discrimination and rights in the session?

10. How will I be able to tell whether the session has been successful?

Table 9.2: Pro forma for tuning in to a groupwork session

Pro forma for written evaluation of a group or session

1. How I prepared for this piece of work.
   (a) What did I hope to contribute to the group?
   (b) In what areas did I wish to improve my practice?
   (c) What was I hoping to learn from others in this piece of groupwork practice?
   (d) How could I have improved on my planning?

2. What was my primary purpose in this piece of work?

3. How successful was I in achieving my main aims?
   (a) Reactions of the groupworkers and members.
   (b) Changes in attitudes.
   (c) Acquisition of knowledge and skills.
   (d) Behavioural change.
   (e) Organisational change.
   (f) Benefits to members and their carers or those for whom they care.

4. What were the main skills that I used?
   (a) What were my strengths in groupwork practice?
   (b) Would I start the group in the same way if I were to do it again?
   (c) Which roles and styles came easily to me and which were more difficult?
   (d) What have I learned about my facilitation style?
   (e) With what sorts of activities did I feel most (and least) comfortable?

5. What knowledge did I employ?
   (a) How well did I use theory?

6. What values were evident in this piece of work?

7. What future learning requirements are indicated by this piece of work?

Table 9.3: Pro forma for written evaluation of a group or session

Having established a benchmark at the beginning of a piece of groupwork, it should be easy for you to revisit the following questions at the end: What has changed? What are the levels of your skills and knowledge now? What do you find easy and difficult now? What did you contribute? . . . and so on.

Here are a few additional questions that you may ask yourself, taken from Whitaker (2001).

- Could I have improved on my planning?

- Would I start the group in the same way if I were to do it again?

- What have I learned about my facilitation style?

- With what sorts of activities do I feel most (and least) comfortable?

- How well did I use theory?

- With what kinds of service users do I like to work?

As with 'tuning in', your practice teacher or supervisor is likely to ask for a written evaluation of your work and again we have included a pro forma (informed by Doel and Sawdon, 1999; Preston-Shoot, 2007) for you to use (Table 9.3).

Finally, we present you with the fourth and final part of the Group Planner. As we need to decide how we will evaluate before the group begins, rather than when it has finished, we have included these evaluation questions in the Planner.

Group Planner

Part four: records and evaluation

Records
What is to be my system of recording and monitoring?

Who is to take responsibility?

Is the system agreed by the agency?

Evaluation
How am I going to evaluate the group:

- as regards effectiveness and stated aims?

- as regards service-user satisfaction?

- as regards referrer satisfaction?

How will I measure effectiveness – what will tell me if anything has changed (for better or for worse)?

ACTIVITY 9.2

We return to the imaginary group for the last time. Use the Group Planner to decide how you intend to record and evaluate the group project.

CHAPTER SUMMARY

- There is a case to be made for gathering evidence of the efficacy and challenges of groupwork for dissemination to a range of different stakeholders. Evidence-based practice leads to the further development of groupwork within social work.

- At the core of evidence-based practice is the discipline of recording and this is an unavoidable task for a number of other reasons. Although challenging, a number of different methods are available, including writing, video and sound recording, and participant journals.

- Evaluation poses some questions and you will need to make choices in terms of your focus, short-term evidence, learning, and behaviour changes and results.

- Students need to provide evidence of competence in groupwork practice. The chapter contains some instruments that may be helpful.

FURTHER READING

Doel, M and Sawdon, C (1999) *The Essential Groupworker.* London: Jessica Kingsley.

This provides a useful chapter on recording and evaluation.

Preston-Shoot, M (1988) A model for evaluating groupwork. *Groupwork*, 2(1): 36–47.

In this article the author proposes eight simple and easy steps as a model for evaluation.

Preston-Shoot, M (2007) *Effective Groupwork.* Basingstoke: Palgrave Macmillan.

This includes a chapter on evaluating and researching groupwork practice.

Riva, MT and Lange, RE (2013) *How Group Leaders can Assess Group Counselling: Group work practice kit.* London: Sage.

This short (63-page) book provides practical guidance on how to establish research designs aimed at evaluating group processes and outcomes and would be a useful resource for any student planning a groupwork research project.

Whitaker, DS (2001) *Using Groups to Help People*, 2nd edition. Hove: Brunner-Routledge.

This contains a chapter on learning from one's own practice and another on practitioner-conducted research.

Conclusion

Our intention in writing this book was to provide you with the basic knowledge and skills that you would need to set up and facilitate a group while on practice learning, and to highlight some important values in undertaking that work. We do not really know why some people are drawn to groupwork and others are not. We personally find it fascinating, interesting, exciting and enjoyable, if sometimes stressful. Other people find it frightening and confusing, but probably not boring. Since you have reached this point in the book, you probably belong to the first group with us, rather than the second. If so, that is good. Groupwork is a difficult method to learn about without actually doing it. It is rather like tying your shoes. It is easier to do than to explain. Nevertheless, we hope we have been successful in making it clearer to you. Two themes have run through the book. One is that the quality of being self-aware is essential to facilitation. The other is the idea that groupwork is a better way of helping people to draw on the fuller resources that are available to them when learning with other people, rather than when working with them individually. In order for this to happen, the resources and strengths that they have need to be recognised, validated and utilised and this is a significant aspect of the facilitation role.

We have taken you through a process of facilitating a groupwork project from beginning to end. The exercises and activities will have helped you transfer your learning from basic knowledge to a deeper understanding. The next step is for you to go out there and get started. We hope we have achieved our aim in providing you with what you need so that you have the confidence to take that step.

Appendix

Subject benchmark for social work

5 Subject knowledge, understanding and skills

Subject knowledge and understanding

5.1   During their degree studies in social work, honours graduates should acquire, critically evaluate, apply and integrate knowledge and understanding in the following core areas of study.

5.1.1 **Social work services, service users and carers**, which include:

- the nature of social work services in a diverse society (with particular reference to concepts such as prejudice, interpersonal, institutional and structural discrimination, empowerment and anti-discriminatory practices);

- the nature and validity of different definitions of, and explanations for, the characteristics and circumstances of service users and the services required by them, drawing on knowledge from research, practice experience, and from service users and carers;

- the focus on outcomes, such as promoting the well-being of young people and their families, and promoting dignity, choice and independence for adults receiving services.

5.1.3 **Values and ethics**, which include:

- the nature, historical evolution and application of social work value.

5.1.4 **Social work theory**, which includes:

- social science theories explaining group and organisational behaviour, adaptation and change;

- models and methods of assessment, including factors underpinning the selection and testing of relevant information, the nature of professional judgement and the processes of risk assessment and decision-making;

- approaches and methods of intervention in a range of settings, including factors guiding the choice and evaluation of these;

- user-led perspectives.

5.1.5 **The nature of social work practice**, which includes:

- the characteristics of practice in a range of community-based and organisational settings within statutory, voluntary and private sectors, and the factors influencing changes and developments in practice within these contexts;

- the nature and characteristics of skills associated with effective practice, both direct and indirect, with a range of service-users and in a variety of settings;

- the processes that facilitate and support service-user choice and independence;

- the place of theoretical perspectives and evidence from international research in assessment and decision-making processes in social work practice;

- the integration of theoretical perspectives and evidence from international research into the design and implementation of effective social work intervention, with a wide range of service users, carers and others;

- the processes of reflection and evaluation, including familiarity with the range of approaches for evaluating service and welfare outcomes, and their significance for the development of practice and the practitioner.

Subject-specific skills and other skills

5.4　Social work honours graduates should acquire and integrate skills in the following core areas.

Problem-solving skills

5.5.1　**Managing problem-solving activities**: honours graduates in social work should be able to plan problem-solving activities, i.e. to:

- think logically, systematically, critically and reflectively;

- plan a sequence of actions to achieve specified objectives, making use of research, theory and other forms of evidence.

5.5.3　**Analysis and synthesis**: honours graduates in social work should be able to analyse and synthesise knowledge gathered for problem-solving purposes, i.e. to:

- assess human situations, taking into account a variety of factors (including the views of participants, theoretical concepts, research evidence, legislation and organisational policies and procedures);

- consider specific factors relevant to social work practice (such as risk, rights, cultural differences and linguistic sensitivities, responsibilities to protect vulnerable individuals and legal obligations).

5.5.4　**Intervention and evaluation**: honours graduates in social work should be able to use their knowledge of a range of interventions and evaluation processes selectively to:

- build and sustain purposeful relationships with people and organisations in community-based, and interprofessional contexts;

- make decisions, set goals and construct specific plans to achieve these, taking into account relevant factors including ethical guidelines;

- negotiate goals and plans with others, analysing and addressing in a creative manner human, organisational and structural impediments to change;

143

- implement plans through a variety of systematic processes that include working in partnership;

- undertake practice in a manner that promotes the well-being and protects the safety of all parties;

- engage effectively in conflict resolution;

- plan, implement and critically review processes and outcomes;

- bring work to an effective conclusion, taking into account the implications for all involved;

- monitor situations, review processes and evaluate outcomes;

- use and evaluate methods of intervention critically and reflectively.

Communication skills

5.6   Honours graduates in social work should be able to communicate clearly, accurately and precisely (in an appropriate medium) with individuals and groups in a range of formal and informal situations, i.e. to:

- make effective contact with individuals and organisations for a range of objectives, by verbal, paper-based and electronic means;

- clarify and negotiate the purpose of such contacts and the boundaries of their involvement;

- listen actively to others, engage appropriately with the life experiences of service users, understand accurately their viewpoint and overcome personal prejudices to respond appropriately to a range of complex personal and interpersonal situations;

- use both verbal and non-verbal cues to guide interpretation;

- identify and use opportunities for purposeful and supportive communication with service users within their everyday living situations;

- make effective preparation for, and lead meetings in a productive way;

- communicate effectively across potential barriers resulting from differences (for example, in culture, language and age).

Skills in working with others

5.7   Honours graduates in social work should be able to work effectively with others, i.e. to:

- involve users of social work services in ways that increase their resources, capacity and power to influence factors affecting their lives;

- consult actively with others, including service users and carers, who hold relevant information or expertise;

- act cooperatively with others, liaising and negotiating across differences such as organisational and professional boundaries and differences of identity or language;

- develop effective helping relationships and partnerships with other individuals, groups and organisations that facilitate change;

- challenge others when necessary, in ways that are most likely to produce positive outcomes.

Skills in personal and professional development

5.8   Honours graduates in social work should be able to:

- advance their own learning and understanding with a degree of independence;

- reflect on and modify their behaviour in the light of experience;

- identify and keep under review their own personal and professional boundaries;

- manage uncertainty, change and stress in work situations;

- handle inter- and intrapersonal conflict constructively;

- understand and manage changing situations and respond in a flexible manner;

- challenge unacceptable practices in a responsible manner;

- take responsibility for their own further and continuing acquisition and use of knowledge and skills.

References

Affirmative Action Agency (1995) *Didn't I Just Say That?* Canberra: Australian Government Publishing Service.

Andrews, DA, Zinger, I, Hoge, RD, Bonta, J, Gendreau, P and Cullen, FT (1990) Does correctional treatment work? A clinically relevant and psychologically informed meta-analysis. *Criminology*, 28(3): 369–404.

Aries, E (1976) *Sex Differences in Small Group Behavior*. Paper presented at the Conference on Sex Roles in American Society: A Psychological Perspective, Troy, New York. ERIC Document ED136089.

Baines, D (ed.) (2007) *Doing Anti-oppressive Practice: Building transformative, politicised social work*. Halifax, NS: Fernwood.

Bandura, A (ed.) (1995) *Self-efficacy in Changing Societies*. New York: Cambridge University Press.

Barry, M (2006) Dispensing (with?) justice: young people's views of the criminal justice system, in Gorman, K, Gregory, M, Hayles, M and Parton, N (eds) *Constructive Work with Offenders.* London: Jessica Kingsley.

Benson, J (2001) *Working More Creatively with Groups*, 2nd edition. London: Routledge.

Beresford, P (2007) *The Changing Roles and Tasks of Social Work from Service Users' Perspectives*. London: Shaping Our Lives National User Network.

Blacklock, N (2003) Gender awareness and the role of the groupworker in programmes for domestic violence perpetrators, in Cohen, M and Mullender, A (eds) *Gender and Groupwork.* London and New York: Routledge.

Branfield, F and Beresford, P (2006) *Making User Involvement Work: Supporting service user networking and knowledge*. York: Joseph Rowntree Foundation. Available online at www.jrf.org.uk/bookshop/eBooks/1410-usernetworking-knowledge.pdf (accessed 6 June 2011).

Brearley, CP (1982) *Risk and Social Work: Hazards and helping*. London: Routledge and Kegan Paul.

Brown, A (1992) *Groupwork*, 3rd edition. Aldershot: Ashgate Publishing.

Brown, A and Mistry, T (1997) Groupwork with mixed membership groups, in Mistry, T and Brown, A (eds) *Race and Groupwork*. London: Whiting and Birch.

Burgess, H (2004) Matrix showing the variations of requirements for the social work degree for the four UK countries. York: Higher Education Academy, Social Policy and Social Work Subject Centre (SWAP). Available online at www.swap.ac.uk/docs/SWReformmatrix.pdf (accessed 4 December 2013).

Burnard, P (1990) *Learning Human Skills: An experiential guide for nurses*. Oxford: Butterworth-Heinemann.

Button, J (1997) Safety in numbers: creating safe space in groupwork. *Self and Society*, 25(2): 4–11.

Cohen, M and Mullender, A (eds) (2003) *Gender and Groupwork.* London and New York: Routledge.

College of Social Work (2012) *Professional Capabilities Framework*. London: College of Social Work. Available online at www.tcsw.org.uk/pcf.aspx (accessed 4 December 2013).

Corden, J and Preston-Shoot, M (1987) *Contracts in Social Work*. Aldershot: Gower.

Corey, G (2004) *Theory and Practice of Group Counselling*. London: Thomson Learning.

Coulshed, V and Orme, J (2006) *Social Work Practice*, 4th edition. Basingstoke: Palgrave Macmillan.

Coyne, RK and Diederich, LT (2013) *What is Group Work? (Group work practice kit)*. London: Sage.

Crago, H (2006) *Couple, Family and Group Work: First steps in interpersonal intervention*. Maidenhead: Open University Press.

Croxton, T (1974) The therapeutic contract in social treatment, in Galsser, P, Sarri, S and Vinter, R (eds) *Individual Change through Small Groups*. New York: The Free Press.

Dalrymple, J and Burke, B (2006) *Anti-oppressive Practice: Social care and the law*, 2nd edition. Buckingham: Open University Press.

Davies, B (1975) *The Use of Groups in Social Work Practice*. London: Routledge and Kegan Paul.

DeLois, K (2003) Genderbending: group work with queer youth, in Cohen, M and Mullender, A (eds) *Gender and Groupwork*. London and New York: Routledge.

DeLucia-Waack, J L and Nitza, A (2013) *Effective Planning for Groups (Group work practice kit)*. London: Sage.

Doel, M (2006) *Using Groupwork*. London: Routledge.

Doel, M and Sawdon, C (1999) *The Essential Groupworker*. London: Jessica Kingsley.

Doherty, P and Enders, P (1993) Women in group psychotherapy, in Alonso, A and Swiller, HI (eds) *Group Therapy in Clinical Practice*. Washington, DC: American Psychiatric Press.

Dominelli, L (2002a) *Anti-oppressive Social Work: Theory and practice*. Basingstoke: Palgrave Macmillan.

Dominelli, L (2002b) *Feminist Social Work Theory and Practice*. Basingstoke: Palgrave Macmillan.

Douglas, T (1978) *Basic Groupwork*. London: Tavistock.

Douglas, T (1991) *A Handbook of Common Groupwork Problems*. London: Tavistock/Routledge.

Douglas, T (1995) *Survival in Groups: The basics for group membership*. Buckingham: Open University Press.

Douglas, T (2000) *Basic Groupwork*, 2nd edition. London: Routledge.

Dutton, J and Kohli, R (1996) The core skills of social work, in Vass, AA (ed.) *Social Work Competences: Core knowledge, values and skills*. London: Sage.

Egan, G (1998) *The Skilled Helper: A problem management approach to helping*, 6th edition. Pacific Grove, CA: Brooks/Cole.

Geldard, K and Geldard, D (2001) *Working with Children in Groups: A handbook for counsellors, educators and community workers*. Basingstoke: Macmillan.

Heron, J (1989) *Six Category Intervention Analysis*. Guildford: University of Surrey.

Heron, J (1999) *The Complete Facilitator's Handbook*. London: Kogan Page.

Heron, J (2001) *Helping the Client: A creative practical guide*. London: Sage.

Herzberg, F, Mausner, B and Snyderman, BB (1959) *The Motivation to Work*. Chichester: John Wiley.

Hodge, J (1985) *Planning for Co-leadership: A practice guide for groupworkers*. Newcastle: University of Newcastle.

Hodgins, DC, El-Guebaly, N and Addington, J (1997) Treatment of substance abusers: single or mixed gender programs? *Addiction*, 92(7): 805–12.

Hogan, C (2003) *Practical Facilitation: A toolkit of techniques*. London: Kogan Page.

Hopmeyer, E and Werk, A (1993) A comparative study of four family bereavement groups. *Groupwork*, 6(2): 107–21.

Houston, G (1990) *The Red Book of Groups and How to Lead Them Better*, 3rd edition. London: The Rochester Foundation.

Jaques, D (2000) *Learning in Groups: A handbook for improving groupwork*, 3rd edition. London: Kogan Page.

Kelly, G (1996) Competence in the analysis of risk, in O'Hagan, K (ed.) *Competence in Social Work Practice*. London: Jessica Kingsley.

Kolb, DA (1984) *Experiential Learning: Experience as the source of learning and development*. Upper Saddle River, NJ: Prentice Hall.

Levine, JM and Moreland, RL (2006) *Small Groups*. Hove: Psychology Press.

Lewin, K (1951) *Field Theory in Social Science*. New York: Harper and Row.

Lewis, E and Gutierrez, L (2003) Intersections of gender, race and ethnicity in groupwork, in Cohen, M and Mullender, A (eds) *Gender and Groupwork*. London and New York: Routledge.

Lindsay, T (2005) Group learning on social work placements. *Groupwork*, 15(1): 61–89.

Lindsay, T (2013) Cognitive behavioural approaches, in Lindsay, T (ed.) *Social Work Intervention*, (2nd edn). London: Sage.

Lindsay, T and Quinn, K (2001) Fairplay in Northern Ireland: towards an anti-sectarian practice. *Probation Journal*, 48(2): 102–9.

Lipsey, M (1992) Juvenile delinquency treatment: a meta-analytic enquiry into the variability of effects, in Cook, T, Cooper, H, Cordray, DS, Hartman, H, Hedges, LV, Light, TL, Louis, TA and Mosteller, F (eds) *Metaanalysis for Explanation: A case book*. New York: Russell Sage.

Manktelow, R and Lindsay, T (2003) *An Evaluation of the Sure Start Services Provided by the Shantallow Community Support Partnership*. Londonderry: Shantallow Community Support Partnership.

Manor, O (1986) The preliminary interview in social groupwork: finding the spiral steps. *Social Work with Groups*, 9(2): 21–39.

Manor, O (1988) Preparing the client for social groupwork: an illustrated framework. *Groupwork*, 2: 100–14.

Manor, O (2000) *Choosing a Groupwork Approach*. London: Jessica Kingsley.

The Members of Women First (2003) Women First: a self-directed group for women with and without learning disabilities – our experiences 1990–99, in Cohen, M and Mullender, A (eds) *Gender and Groupwork*. London and New York: Routledge.

Mullender, A (2003) Conclusion: where does this leave us?, in Cohen, M and Mullender, A (eds) *Gender and Groupwork*. London and New York: Routledge.

National Coalition Building Institute (NCBI) (2003) *Principles into Practice: Strengthening leadership for a diverse society.* Washington, DC: National Coalition Building Institute.

Parker, J (2004) *Effective Practice Learning in Social Work.* Exeter: Learning Matters.

Parton, N and O'Byrne, P (2000) *Constructive Social Work: Towards a new practice.* Basingstoke: Palgrave Macmillan.

Phillips, J (2006) *Groupwork in Social Care.* London: Jessica Kingsley.

Poole, MS (1981) Decision development in small groups I: a comparison of two models. *Communication Monographs*, 48: 1–24.

Preston-Shoot, M (1989) Using contracts in groupwork. *Groupwork*, 2(1): 36–47.

Preston-Shoot M (2007) *Effective Groupwork*, 2nd edition. Basingstoke: BASW/Macmillan.

Prince, K (1996) *Boring Records? Communication, speech and writing in social work.* London: Jessica Kingsley.

Rapin, LS and Crowell, JL (2013) *How to Form a Group (Group work practice kit).* London: Sage.

Riva, MT (2013) Supervision of group leaders, in DeLucia-Waak, JL, Kalodner, CR and Riva, MT (eds) *Handbook of Group Counselling and Psychotherapy.* Thousand Oaks, CA: Sage.

Rogers, CR (1957) The necessary and sufficient conditions of therapeutic personality change. *Journal of Consulting Psychology*, 21(2): 95–103.

Rogers, CR (1970) *Carl Rogers on Encounter Groups.* New York: Harper Row.

Scally, M and Lindsay, T (1997) *Teaching and Assessing Groupwork in a Social Work Context.* Paper presented to the Seventh European Groupwork Symposium, Cork, July 1997.

Schimmel, C and Jacobs, E (2013) *How to Select and Apply Change Strategies in Groups (Group work practice kit).* London: Sage.

Schutz, WC (1958) *FIRO-B: A three dimensional theory of interpersonal behaviour.* New York: Reinhart.

Schwartz, W (1971) Introduction: on the use of groups in social work practice, in Schwartz, W and Zalba, SR (eds) *The Practice of Groupwork.* New York: Columbia University Press.

Shaping Our Lives National User Network (SOL) (2007) *Definitions.* London: Shaping Our Lives. Available online at www. shapingourlives.org.uk (accessed 7 July 2011).

Sharry, J (2001) *Solution Focused Groupwork.* London: Sage.

Smith-Lovin, L and Brody, C (1989) Interruptions in group discussions: the effects of gender and group composition. *American Sociological Review*, 54: 424–35.

Thompson, N (2006) *Anti-discriminatory Practice*, 4th edition. Basingstoke: Palgrave Macmillan.

Trevithick, P (2005a) The knowledge base of groupwork and its importance within social work. *Groupwork*, 15(2): 80–107.

Trevithick, P (2005b) *Social Work Skills: A practice handbook*, 2nd edition. Buckingham: Open University Press.

Trevithick, P (2006) The place of groupwork in the new social work degree. *Groupwork*, 16(2): 3–7.

Tuckman, BW (1965) Developmental sequence in small groups. *Psychological Bulletin*, 63: 384–99.

Turner, M and Beresford, P (2005) *User Controlled Research: Its meanings and potential: final report*. Eastleigh: Involve.

Vinter, RD (1967) Program activities: an analysis of their effects upon participant behaviour, in Vinter, RD (ed.) *Readings in Group Work Practice*. Ann Arbor, MI: Campus Publishers.

Ward, D (2002) Groupwork, in Adams, R, Dominelli, L and Payne, M (eds) *Social Work: Themes, issues and critical debates*, 2nd edition. Basingstoke: Palgrave Macmillan.

Whitaker, DS (1985) *Using Groups to Help People*. London: Routledge and Kegan Paul.

Whitaker, DS (2001) *Using Groups to Help People*, 2nd edition. Hove: Brunner-Routledge.

Williams, M (1966) Limitations, fantasies and security operations of beginning group psycho-therapists. *International Journal of Group Psychotherapy*, 16: 150–62.

Wilson, A and Beresford, P (2000) Anti-oppressive practice: emancipation or appropriation? *British Journal of Social Work*, 30: 553–73.

Index